What is Art?

Art and Law

Volumes published in this Brill Research Perspectives title are listed at *brill.com/rpal*

What is Art?

The Question of Definition Reloaded

By

Tiziana Andina

BRILL

LEIDEN | BOSTON

This paperback book edition is simultaneously published as issue 1.2 (2017) of *Art and Law*, 10.1163/24684309-12340002.

Library of Congress Control Number: 2017958099

Typeface for the Latin, Greek, and Cyrillic scripts: "Brill". See and download: brill.com/brill-typeface.

ISBN 978-90-04-36141-6 (paperback)
ISBN 978-90-04-36142-3 (e-book)

This book is printed on acid-free paper and produced in a sustainable manner.

Contents

What is Art?
The Question of Definition Reloaded

Tiziana Andina
University of Turin, Italy
tiziana.andina@unito.it

Abstract

'What is art?' is one of the classic questions that philosophy has addressed over the ages, from the ancients to today. Taking as its starting point debates over the various definitions of art found in history, this article presents and discusses some of the major theories offered by both the analytic and continental traditions. It then looks at the theoretical reasons that led twentieth-century philosophy to reopen the question of definition, and in many cases inquire into the ontology of art itself. Finally, a series of considerations are addressed to help shift the problem of definition onto a new plane, one that is able to respond to the challenges of the performing and participatory arts, which more than any other form of art present particularly unconventional ontologies.

Keywords

art – definition – aboutness – normativity – medium – emotions

1 The Problem of Definition: Classical Questions

That the question of defining art should be of any interest to philosophy may strike us, initially, as rather odd. Why, after all, is it necessary to define art? Why should we concern ourselves with developing a more detailed and appropriate understanding of art—by defining it, for example, as a concept in more precise terms? Roughly speaking, we know what we are talking about when we refer to things like pictures, musical works, novels, and pop music, and we have learned, in many cases, to distinguish performance from ordinary action. Even the bizarre objects we come across in contemporary art museums around the world no longer stir in us any particular sense of astonishment.

 | DOI 10.1163/9789004361423_001

Nevertheless, philosophy has often turned to the question of defining art, and it has done so broadly for two main reasons. First of all, art has always been a domain of specific application for philosophy, in the sense that art raises numerous questions of a philosophical nature. Philosophy has always treated works of art as objects of curiosity, as much as, or even more than, other objects that populate the world. Just how compelling art is for philosophy is shown immediately by the many different aspects of art that have become the object of study. These aspects range from questions that lie at the boundary of philosophy and psychology (why have humans in all ages and of all cultures felt the need to express themselves through art?), to matters of an ontological nature (what kind of thing is a work of art?), through to practical-functional concerns (what is the purpose of art?), and how we formulate value judgements about art (what does it mean to judge a work of art a masterpiece?), and so forth. Hence, it is not just the concept of art in general but also objects of art that have repeatedly engaged and challenged philosophical thought. For the most part, the domain of art has always been treated as a specific domain, with roots that lie deep in the religious sphere (Nietzsche 2008), but which then diverges and spreads, marking the intellectual development attained by a culture, while at the same time continuing to preserve in the body of art the vestiges of that ancient bond. That is why, for example, philosophy has focused extensively on reconstructing the passage from the concept of presentation, which is of a religious nature, to the concept of representation, where the idea of a divinity appearing on stage and revealing itself through the bodies of those who venerate it publicly gives way to the idea of a divinity who is evoked through the capacity for representation of actors—actors who do not bring the divinity to life through their bodies but signify it in more complex and sophisticated ways (Danto 1981).

Secondly, philosophy has concerned itself with the question of what it is that leads us to take art as a whole seriously, and even remain captivated by it. This typically happens with certain kinds of art, such as theatre, film, or literature, which potentially are especially powerful in their capacity to elicit an emotional response from the audience. How is it possible for us to be terrified watching *Suspiria* by Dario Argento, or to be moved reading the story of Paolo and Francesca in the *Divine Comedy*? Or to feel a boundless sadness listening to the music of Max Richter, before discovering, through the title of the work, *Sarajevo*, that the notes of that particular piece capture and convey at a formal and emotional level the meaning of a devastating destruction and grief? In short, we experience a vast range of emotions when faced with a work of art. What is surprising in this is that all those emotions are authentic, in the sense that we, as spectators who are sensitive to art, cannot help but experience those emotions for real, even though their nuances may be different for each of us. That happens even though we all know full well that the characters in *Suspiria* do not exist and have never existed, and that Paolo and Francesca were reinvented by Dante for the purpose of his narrative and so in a sense they never really existed, and they certainly no longer exist at the moment when the story of their love moves us to tears. It is, of course, likely that real people once lived who experienced similar mishaps, or who exhibited similar personality traits to those of the characters of those stories, but in any case they are just stories, tales that are the fruit of our imagination. The victims of Sarajevo may have left their trace in collective memory and history books, but we are well aware that there is no real difference between the emotion we feel over Paolo and Francesca and the emotion evoked by the victims of Sarajevo. Both sentiments are elicited by objects that have a peculiar form of existence (in this case they are works of art) and which may or may not refer to objects that belong to the world—objects that exist or once existed, or objects that have never existed at all. None of this, however, would appear to make any difference, not at least in relation to the substantiality of the emotions they evoke.[1] Our fear, pity, and terror remain ever present in our minds and in our guts, regardless of whether the object that elicits them exists or ever existed.

There is a paradox in the fact that our emotions do not distinguish between real and fictional objects which leads us to another, arguably more interesting paradox, which in literature is known as the 'paradox of tragedy'. Aristotle addressed the paradox of tragedy in his *Rhetoric*, where he identified in tragedy its essential ability to arouse two negative emotions, pity and fear (Aristotle 2007, II 5 II 8). That the two emotions are negative should be stressed, in the sense that they are emotions that depress the spirit,[2] which leads us spontaneously to ask why we seek out such emotions and the objects that provoke them. Why do we torture ourselves by watching a horror film? Is it that the fear we experience watching a horror film is somehow different to the fear we feel in experiencing the *same* scene or a very similar scene in the real world?

Perhaps here we should reflect on what we mean by the 'same'. The two sentiments may be very similar but they are not really the same. Imagine watching

1 For a more in-depth discussion of negative sentiments in art, which in literature is known as the paradox of tragedy, see Levinson (2014).

2 These two emotions would go on to see remarkable success in the history of philosophical thought. To cite just a couple of the better-known examples, fear constitutes the basis on which Hobbes developed his political thought (2012), whereas pity, or more specifically compassion, is the sentiment that Nietzsche (1997) posits as the foundation for the transvaluation of values in Christianity.

a play in which a mother plans to kill her children. Assuming everybody in the audience is aware of being at the theatre, nobody would stand up and try to stop the mother. They would probably feel a sense of fear, but not excessively, in the sense that they can draw on any number of stratagems to keep their fear in check. They could, for instance, try and distract themselves—after all, nobody is really going to get hurt, neither the audience, nor the mother, let alone the children. Or they could even stop and examine the nature of that sentiment in the spirit of a psychologist. Vice versa, if we saw a woman attempting to kill her child, we would have a material and moral obligation to try and stop her. We would not be able to think of anything else, or at least we would not be able to divert our thoughts towards things not directly connected with the event—and we would certainly not be able to reflect in any specific way on the fact of 'being afraid'. Undoubtedly, we would be afraid, among other things, but we would be paying attention to what the woman is doing, what we should be doing, and how to avert the tragedy. So Aristotle was fully justified in wanting to examine the specificity of the fear elicited by art, of a sentiment that is a specific variant of the typical fear that we experience in everyday life and which finds in art its own dimension enabling specific expression. It is, therefore, plausible to hold that the fear that grips us in witnessing a murder is something very similar to the fear we experience in watching a drama (whether on stage or on screen) which draws on fear, but which is not exactly the same as fear. Rather, what it might be is a variation of a primary emotion (the fear we experience in everyday life when faced with a real or presumed danger), which is an emotion of precise biological origin. The distinctive element of the fear elicited by fictional situations is the fact that—and this is certainly the case that Aristotle had in mind—those who experience it are almost always aware that they are witnessing a fictional representation. Hence, they know they are observing a situation in which there is really no concrete reason to feel a sense of fear. Thus it is easy to assume that it is the information that we draw from the context that allows us to channel precisely not so much what we feel, the emotion, but the emotive and cognitive response that we attach to that emotion. The fictional context is, by definition, a space that benefits from rather particular properties and characteristics, such as, for example, the fact that the audience generally only passively partake in it as observers. That is, the situation of the audience is that of observing the action, in which they are involved only as observers. Granting, therefore, that the audience experience fear, and considering that fear is an emotion of a contextual kind, i.e., it depends closely on the context in which is arises, there are compelling elements to favour the theory that fear in a fictional and artistic context is something that resembles the same emotion experienced in a non-fictional context. Nevertheless, we associate different contextual properties to the two sentiments, which gives us two different variants of one and the same emotion. Hence, we have two similar emotions, which in absolute terms means they are different emotions.

1.1 *The Problem of Definition: Questions of Contemporary Art*

These issues open up debates that have become classics in philosophy.[3] What has brought the question of the definition of art back to prominence, however, and which should be stressed, is that the arts in the twentieth century deliberately and systematically altered the terms of the relationship between the space of ordinary reality and fictional space, raising new questions and framing old ones in radically new terms. Numerous examples can be given that are interesting from a theoretical point of view. Many have become classics in the exemplification of the theoretical questions raised by contemporary art. Here we shall look at and illustrate only some, to then address, in the following pages, the issues they raise and examine how they affect the question of definition, which is what interests us here. Let us begin with the celebrated case of the Romanian sculptor Constantin Brâncuși.

1.1.1 "Does it look like a bird to you?" Art as Mimesis of the Real World

In 1926, Constantin Brâncuși arrived in the United States with his sculpture *Bird in Space*. Brâncuși was travelling with the sculpture to exhibit it in what was fast becoming a world capital of contemporary art, New York City. To facilitate its transport, the sculpture was dismantled, with the pedestal separated from the body of the work. At U.S. Customs, the officers tasked with inspecting incoming goods rejected the artist's declaration, which classified the object as a work of art, and instead decided to classify *Bird in Space* as a mere kitchen utensil. Specifically, they decided that what they were dealing with was a knife, a simple utilitarian object.

Before examining the consequences of the Customs officers' decision, it will help to stress a point made by Bernard Edelman (2011, p. 21). Copyright in law is a concept based on a very particular idea. A maker can sell something, x, which she herself has created. Yet in the case of objects covered by copyright, it is believed and accepted that in selling the object, the maker does not completely alienate the relative property rights. In fact, the maker retains a monopoly over reproductions. If instead we think of when we sell land or a house, we cannot help but notice a certain incongruity in this. A work of art is evidently perceived to be something rather different when compared to an ordinary object,

---

3 For a framework of the debate over theories addressing the question of definition see Abell (2012, 671–691) Andina (2013), Carroll (2000), Freeland (2001), and Lopes (2014).

something which is different not just from an ontological point of view, but very often in terms of its value. That is why we accept the idea that the maker continues to enjoy rights over the object despite the fact she has sold it. In other words, if I purchase a piece of land, I have the right to exploit it and enjoy its fruits, but if I purchase a book, I cannot reproduce it for sale and earn a profit. Nor can I modify its parts, or parts of the story if it is a literary work, without the prior consent of the maker. That privilege demands something in exchange, which Edelman identifies in what the arts can offer society, namely, the promise of benefits for users in terms of culture and education. In other words, it as though the state and education system granted broad rights in exchange for broad benefits for the cultural sphere and education of its citizens. That is why the preamble of the Massachusetts Copyright Act of March 1783 states:

> Whereas the improvement of knowledge, the progress of civilization, the publick weal of the Commonwealth, and the advancement of human happiness, greatly depend on the efforts of learned and ingenious persons in the various arts and sciences: As the principal encouragement such persons can have to make great and beneficial exertions of this nature, must exist in the legal security of the fruits of their study and industry to themselves, and as such security is one of the natural rights of all men, there being no property more peculiarly man's own than that which is produced by the labour of his mind.
>
> CRAWFORD 1975, 14

Much the same spirit is shown in the New Jersey Act for the Promotion and Encouragement of Literature, passed in 1783, in Article 1, Section 8, Clause 8 of the Constitution of the United States, and in various rulings of the U.S. Supreme Court.

Now, given such a framework, it is fairly clear to see why the U.S. Customs officers were indeed unable to decipher and correctly classify the object that arrived in Customs, an object that did not at all look like a traditional work of art. And so they recorded the object as a mere kitchen utensil. The officers' decision has two important implications. The first is that the decision, regardless of the officers' actual intentions, was of significance at the artistic level. From being considered a work of art, as instructed by the artist, *Bird in Space* was reclassified as a mere kitchen utensil, which means, *inter alia,* that the object possessed no artistic value and that its economic value was on par with utilitarian objects of a certain kind. The second implication is, instead, legal. The customs officers levied a customs duty on the object at the ordinary rate applied to utilitarian objects, which is significant from an economic point of view because while utilitarian objects are subject to ordinary taxation, works of art enjoy a facilitated regime. So, whatever their intentions, the fact is that the Customs officers' decision ended up having broad implications at the value level.

The affair led Brâncuși to bring an action in court for the recovery of the duty, in a celebrated case that would come to set an important precedent: *Brâncuși v. United States.*[4] Previously, before the Brâncuși case, the court had already addressed similar questions in the 1916 case *United States v. Olivotti & Co.* In that case the court had ruled in accordance with the Tariff Act, providing a definition of sculpture that was absolutely traditional and, in many respects, conservative:

> Sculpture is that branch of the free fine arts which chisels or carves in stone or other solid material or models in clay or other plastic substance for subsequent reproduction by carving or casting, imitations of natural objects, chiefly the human form, and represents such objects in their true proportions of length, breadth and thickness, or of length and breadth only.
>
> HARTSHORNE 1986, 96

In his commentary of the ruling, Forbes Watson observed how the court's objective was twofold, and how it failed in both. The first aim was of a pragmatic nature and consisted in preventing utilitarian objects being passed off as works of art in Customs. The second was to provide a definition of sculpture. In specific cases, however, that definition would prove unserviceable, as if it were taken seriously it would exclude any work of art that was not of classical inspiration, which is obviously not practicable. The fine line of distinction which we should not lose sight of, therefore, was the line separating manufactured implements, created to serve a purpose, and works of art, which, on the contrary, only serve to imitate reality—which means they serve no purpose at all, or no concrete purpose. Nevertheless, paragraph 1704 of the Tariff Act did in fact provide guidance to the court, as it exempted from duties:

> Original paintings in oil, mineral, water, or other colors, pastels, original drawings and sketches in pen, ink, pencil, or water colors, artists' proof etchings unbound, and engravings and woodcuts unbound, original sculptures or statuary, including not more than two replicas or

4 The affair is described in detail in Biro (2003).

> reproductions of the same; but the terms "sculpture" and "statuary" as used in this paragraph shall be understood to include professional productions of sculptors only, whether in round or in relief, in bronze, marble, stone, terra cotta, ivory, wood, or metal, or whether cut, carved, or otherwise wrought by hand from the solid block or mass of marble, stone, or alabaster, or from metal, or cast in bronze or other metal or substance, or from wax or plaster, made as the professional productions of sculptors only; and the words "painting" and "sculpture" and "statuary" as used in this paragraph shall not be understood to include any articles of utility, nor such as are made wholly or in part by stenciling or any other mechanical process; and the words "etchings," "engravings," and "woodcuts" as used in this paragraph shall be understood to include only such as are printed by hand from plates or blocks etched or engraved with hand tools and not such as are printed from plates or blocks etched or engraved by photochemical or other mechanical processes.
>
> *Tariff Act of 1922, with Index*, H.R. 7456, WASHINGTON: GOVERNMENT PRINTING OFFICE, P. 84

The idea that the Tariff Act gives of art work is thus quite simple. Art is tied to originality, expressed in various forms and with various media. The objects should not be produced in large quantities, hence they may not be mass produced. Sculptures, in particular, may only be made of certain materials or alloys and crafted by professional sculptors. Moreover, and this was the point that was probably most important for the lawmakers, they may not be made using mechanical processes. Essentially, works of art had to be the outcome of creative processes that were clearly distinct from industrial production processes. Industrial production produced objects designed for a purpose, whereas art was free to perform a function or, if one preferred, it could be completely and utterly useless.

Turning back to Brâncuși, among the first to realize that the case was interesting from many points of view was the photographer who had purchased the sculpture, Edward Steichen, who related the affair to Gertrude Vanderbilt Whitney, founder of the Whitney Museum of American Art in New York. Realizing that the case would set a formidable judicial precedent, Whitney offered to cover the legal fees for the court case. Six witnesses testified for Brâncuși: Edward Steichen, the sculptor Jacob Epstein, the editor of the magazine *The Arts*, the editor of *Vanity Fair*, the director of the Brooklyn Museum of Art, and the art critic Henry McBride. Marcus Higginbotham represented U.S. Customs. The United States government also called two witnesses, the sculptors Robert Aitken and Thomas Jones. The government defended the actions of the U.S. Customs officers by citing the precedent set by the 1916 case *United States v. Olivotti & Co.*, in which the court had ruled that only articles recognised as imitations of objects of nature qualified as art. The following extracts from the proceedings are revealing in many ways.

> JUSTICE WAITE: What do you call this?
> STEICHEN: I use the same term the sculptor did, *oiseau*, a bird.
> WAITE: What makes you call it a bird, does it look like a bird to you?
> STEICHEN: It does not look like a bird, but I feel that it is a bird, it is characterized by the artist as a bird.
> WAITE: Simply because he [the artist] called it a bird, does that make it a bird to you?
> WAITE: If you would see it on the street you never would think of calling it a bird, would you?
> JUSTICE YOUNG: If you saw it in the forest you would not take a shot at it?
> STEICHEN: No, your Honour.
>
> ROWELL AND PALEOLOGUE 1999, 20

Clearly, what the judge was questioning was whether something could be considered a work of art if it does not convey aspects of the real world, that is, if it does not substantially resemble reality. We shall call this the *mimetic prejudice* of the traditional theory of art. As the proceedings continued, a second prejudice became clearly evident, which we shall call the *prejudice in favour of beauty*.[5] Let us return to the transcript.

> Q. You consider from the training you have had and based on your experience you had in these different schools and galleries—you consider that a work of art?
> A. I certainly do.
> Q. When you say you consider that a work of art, will you kindly tell me why?
> A. Well, it pleases my sense of beauty, gives me a feeling of pleasure. Made by a sculptor, it has to me a great many elements, but consists in itself as a beautiful object. To me it is a work of art.
> Q. So if we had a brass rail, highly polished, curved in more or less harmonious circles, it would be a work of art?
> A. It might become a work of art.

---

5 Both prejudices persist in the modern concept of art that emerges from Batteaux's theory, which notoriously holds that through imitation, the fine arts aim to create beauty.

Q. Whether it was made by a sculptor or made by a mechanic?
A. A mechanic cannot make beautiful work.
Q. Do you mean to tell us that Exhibit One, if formed up by a mechanic—that is, a first class mechanic with a file and polishing tools—could not polish that article up?
A. He could polish it up but he cannot conceive of the object. That is the whole point. He cannot conceive those particular lines which give it its individual beauty. That is the difference between a mechanic and an artist; he [the mechanic] cannot conceive as an artist.
JUSTICE WAITE: If he can conceive, then he would cease to be a mechanic and become an artist?
WITNESS: Would become an artist; that is right.

ROWELL AND PALEOLOGUE 1999, 28

Two things clearly emerge from the cross-examination of the witness. The first is how the question of beauty, or the idea that art is a vehicle for beauty, was considered a fundamental element in identifying a work of art. Ultimately, it was unthinkable for a work of art not to exhibit beauty. The idea was that only art can show true beauty and only the artist is capable of effectively conveying it, of expressing it fully. The other fundamental element is tied to the technical skills that enable a work of art to be produced. Here, the idea was that such skills were not in themselves sufficient to identify an artist and an art work, as ultimately even a skilled mechanic should be able to polish a piece of metal perfectly and in an aesthetically fine way. Something else was needed and that something probably lay in the idea that the artist, and only the artist, had in mind throughout the creative and production process. The words of the editor-in-chief of *Vanity Fair*, under cross-examination, speak clearly:

Q. If you took a brass rail perfectly curved and symmetrically formed, highly polished, it would appeal to you also as a work of art?
A. No, Sir. If it appeared some great artist made the rail …
Q. Suppose you did not know who made it?
A. That would not affect it at all.
Q. It would make no difference at all if so far as its artistic quality is concerned or its appealing quality, or its harmonious balance, form, etc., if made by a mechanic or made by a sculptor?
A. If it is beautiful it could not have been made by a mechanic

ROWELL AND PALEOLOGUE 1999, 39

The court closed the case on 26th November, 1928 ruling in favour of Brâncuşi. *Bird in Space was a work of art.* In many respects, the decision acknowledged the end of a conception of art based on beauty, on mimesis, and, finally, on a certain mimetic function of art. The grounds for the ruling stated:

> The object now under consideration is shown to be for purely ornamental purposes, its use being the same as that of any piece of sculpture of the old masters. It is beautiful and symmetrical in outline, and while some difficulty might be encountered in associating it with a bird, it is nevertheless pleasing to look at and highly ornamental. And as we hold under the evidence that it is the original production of a professional sculptor and is in fact a piece of sculpture and a work of art according to the authorities above referred to, we sustain the protest and find that it is entitled to free entry under paragraph 1704, supra.
>
> ROWELL AND PALEOLOGUE 1999, 15

It is important to grasp the reasons that led the U.S. Customs officers to reject Brâncuşi's claims. To begin with, those reasons were evidently connected with how art was commonly perceived in the United States. If we examine the depositions made by the parties involved in the court case, what actually emerges is the widespread conception that was held of art, a conception that was eminently mimetic and strictly dependent, at times in contradictory ways, on the idea of beauty and the means of its production by someone who necessarily should possess abilities that a craftsman does not possess. Essentially, art was understood as a means of achieving the beautiful mimesis of parts of reality. It is clear that *Bird in Space* seriously challenged both the nature and the function of art. Moreover, even the role of the artist must have appeared, to the Customs officers, to be brought into question by Brâncuşi's work. What, exactly, was the role of the artist? To create objects? That, however, was traditionally the task reserved to craftsmen. A sculptor like Brâncuşi could most certainly be considered a craftsman, but we are not inclined to consider all craftsmen to be artists. And then, assuming that the purpose of art is to imitate reality, how far can it depart from the model? In other words, how creative, original, and inventive can art be? What did the Customs officers mean when they claimed that *Bird in Space* did not look at all like a bird? What kind of bird was it meant to resemble? Perhaps the idea of a bird, its stereotype? If a work of art that represents a bird, as in Brâncuşi's case, is in no way similar to the idea of a bird, is the artist entitled to insist that his creation refers to a bird? The U.S. Customs officers were unprepared to accept a way of thinking of art, in this specific case of sculpture, as proposed by Brâncuşi, and the result was that they adopted a normative and prescriptive stance aimed at defending a more common conception of art—*that was not a work of art and, in that case at least, Brâncuşi probably could not be considered an artist*. Ultimately, there could not be much room for discretion in imitating a bird if art was chiefly to have an educational purpose, that is, if people were meant to be able to recognise in the work the fundamental characteristics that identify the represented object.

As Edelman rightly observes, the degree of freedom granted to art and the artist in European culture and in American culture was profoundly different. Their respective laws provide a perfect litmus test demonstrating the differences. In French law, for example, a work of art is strictly tied to the artist in very much irresolvable ways, and considers it a right of the person. In other words, works of art have more to do with people than with things, which obviously may strike us as quite bizarre if we consider the simple fact that works of art are things and not people, but if we bear in mind that we usually have moral obligations towards art works and art in general, the point is, perhaps, clearer.[6] The legal sphere typically encompasses two major domains: the domain of relationships and the acts that derive from them; and the domain of things. The possession of things is dependent on property rights that permit their use. In this framework, works of art have a rather special nature, as revealed first of all by the ontology identifying them. A book, for example, is of course an object, or an artefact. It is composed of numerous printed pages, bound together to form a single object, in different ways. Yet to understand the specificity of a literary work, or what makes a book a work of art, it does not suffice to focus on the properties of the artefact, of the physical object and book. In that sense, a literary work of art cannot be reduced to the material properties of the object that identifies it—indeed, the set of those properties in no way identifies the work. Whereas, on the contrary, the set of material properties that identify an object as a 'piece of land' identify the piece of land. As perfectly underscored by law, there is 'something more', even if not exactly identified, that distinguishes a book object from the work of art 'contained' in the book. Now, while the point may seem intuitively clear for literary and musi-

6 An interesting discussion of this point is provided by Anthony Cross (2017). Cross argues that although it is uncontroversial that obligation constrains our engagement with art, in the form of obligations to other people, including artists, audiences, and owners of art works such obligations do not derive from the supposed moral rights of art works. Rather, he argues that these obligations are instances of duties of love: obligations that one incurs in virtue of loving some object, be it a person or, in this case, an art work.

cal works of art, it becomes much more complicated when we apply it to the visual arts. We might understand it well for a canvas, which in a certain sense is equivalent to a blank page. But what about things like colours, which are also material properties? Are they distinct from the work of art? Do they identify it? And what is their relationship with the canvas, i.e., with the material medium of the work?

Copyright, as Edelman appropriately observes, emerges from the effort to separate works of art from the domain of things. Works are not like other things, and so they can be treated and protected differently to how other types of things are. Essentially, it is not possible, and should not be possible, to separate a work from its maker, whereas it is always possible, in practice and by law, to alienate the property of land—you just sell it. A work of art can be sold, and artists sell their works constantly to gallery owners, museums, publishers, and private buyers, yet in a sense there is something in the work can never be alienated from its maker. It is not possible to alter, either in a major or most minor way, the *Divine Comedy*, not even after more than seven centuries have passed since the author wrote it, and not even if it were the first, original publisher of the book to claim the right to do so. The *Divine Comedy* will always be just as Dante conceived and wrote it because it is part of Dante, a continuation of Dante's world, and as such it belongs more to him than to us. Kant grasped the point perfectly when he wrote:

> *on the one hand*, a book is a corporeal *artifact* [...] that can be reproduced (by someone in legitimate possession of a copy of it), so that there is a *right to a thing* with regard to it. *On the other hand*, a book is also a mere discourse of the publisher to the public, which the publisher may not repeat publicly without having a mandate from the author to do so [...] and this is a *right against a person*. The error consists in mistaking one of these rights for the other.
>
> KANT 1996, 437–8

Part of the complexity faced in any attempt to define art arises precisely from this aspect, from the specificity of a category, that of art, which takes many particular forms and whose ontology pertains in part to material objects and in part to people. Such objects, therefore, populate a slice of reality that straddles the world of things and the world of people and which, moreover, is relatively unstable, in the sense that it endlessly produces exemplifications that are new and, in some cases, completely different to those constituting the historical set of exemplifications to which new works are added.

2 Metaphysical Issues: The Transfiguration of a Box

A number of years later, another work of art appeared before Customs officers. This time it was Canadian Customs and the artist involved was Andy Warhol. *Brillo Box* is a famous series of boxes that Andy Warhol exhibited at the Stable Gallery in New York in 1964. *Brillo Box* is an object with a background, one of great philosophical interest, which lies behind the story of the art work. Before becoming a work of art, the Brillo box was a carton designed by James Harvey, an artist who designed commercial objects to make a living. It was Harvey who conceived the first exemplar of the Brillo box, which would be manufactured as packaging for the sale of soap pads. The box designed by Harvey is very similar, but not identical, that is, it is not indiscernible from the box created by Andy Warhol's Factory. The two objects look so much alike, however, that it would have come as no surprise had Harvey sued for plagiarism—not from a common sense point of view, at any rate.

The work was brought to Canada in 1965 by the art merchant Jerrold Morris. Once again, the Customs officers looked at the boxes and considered them mere grocery boxes, objects of utility or, more precisely, merchandise, and levied the corresponding duty. It was an easy mistake to make. Supermarkets around the world were full of Brillo boxes, where they contained useful soap pads for washing pots and pans. To resolve the dispute, an expert was specially called in, Dr Charles Comfort, director of the National Gallery of Canada. After seeing photographs of Warhol's boxes, Comfort agreed with the Customs officers that Brillo Box was merely merchandise and as such should be taxed. Today we know that *Brillo Box* is considered a sculpture, and so *a fortiori* it is considered a work of art. What is interesting from a philosophical point of view is to understand how we have come to consider possible what in many ways is very much a transfiguration, one that transforms an everyday object of utility into a work of art. A box designed and manufactured for the sale of soap has become a work of art emblematic of an era.

2.1 *More Metaphysical Issues: Intermittent Art*

Let us now turn to a third case of art encountering Customs, this time in the European Union. *Icons*, a work by Dan Flavin, was shipped to Europe from the United States to be exhibited in London. The work is made of neon lights, specifically six fluorescent neon tubes and six lighting devices made of plastic, which form a light sculpture. The installation piece is obviously the fruit of Flavin's mind and its activation requires instructions provided by the artist. The devices are separate and designed for vertical assembly, in which the neon tubes are then assembled. When switched on, the installation emits two alternating shades of white light. The sculpture was dismantled for transport and the neon tubes packed separately in crates. Imagine the scene when the Customs officers opened the crates to inspect their contents. All they found was lighting material, objects literally lacking any particular aesthetic quality. As in our past cases, they decided to classify the neon tubes as utilitarian objects, specifically light fittings.

What ensued was a dispute between the gallery representing the artist and the European Union. The judge ruled that Flavin's work could not be classified as sculpture because it was not the installation itself that constituted an art work but the luminous effects of the installation, namely, the play of lights created by the neon tubes. As it was not even an object of antiquarian interest, the work was to be taxed as an ordinary light fitting. Once again, the judge handed down a ruling of interest not only for its legal precedent, but for its important metaphysical implications. After a lengthy and complicated dispute, the decision established that *Icon* was a work of art only when the installation was switched on. That means, for example, that the ontological status of the neon tubes is different depending on what they are doing. If they are dismantled and switched off, they are utilitarian objects, which is something of a paradox as nobody is actually using them at that moment. On the contrary, if they are assembled and switched on, in that case they are a work of art, which again highlights a certain inconsistency, as it is only when they serve their utilitarian purpose of lighting, i.e., when they are switched on, that the judge decided they should be treated as a work of art.

Flavin's work, as in many other cases of contemporary art, indirectly raises a series of important questions of a metaphysical nature. One of those questions, for instance, concerns the identity of objects. That those questions could be raised in the case at hand was made possible by the physical structure of the work, which in many ways was unconventional and atypical, especially when compared to more traditional works of visual art. Thus we have that one and the same object should be judged in different ways, and classified accordingly under different ontological categories, depending on whether it is switched on or off. Yet the *Mona Lisa* does not change status when in transit from one museum to another—nobody would labour under the illusion that at one moment it is a work of art, and a table top over which to sip tea the next.

2.2 *Other Metaphysical Puzzles*

Customs adventures apart, there is no shortage of examples of works of art that raise questions of philosophical import. In this section, we shall look at a few that can be considered exemplary.

Fountain (1917) is a work by the French artist Marcel Duchamp, which he submitted, under a pseudonym, for an art competition called by the Society for Independent Arts. The work is a urinal purchased from a store in Manhattan and signed by the artist, using the chosen pseudonym, without altering or changing any of the physical properties of the object. In this case, the utilitarian object coincides quite literally with the work of art. That is to say, we know that none of the properties of the object that Duchamp purchased in the Manhattan store were altered or modified by the artist. Then again, the principle of the identity of indiscernibles speaks clearly on this point: if every property of x is also a property of y, and vice versa, then x and y are identical. In our case, every physical property of the urinal is manifestly a property of *Fountain*, and vice versa, hence we must necessarily conclude that the urinal and *Fountain* are the same thing. *Fountain* and the urinal thus share all their properties, which is precisely the point, as common sense would lead us to believe that works of art share certain properties with ordinary objects (such as, classically, their being artefacts), but do not share all of them. That means that the class of art works is supposed to exhibit different properties, or different sets of properties, compared to the class of ordinary objects. *Fountain* shows the exact opposite, without, however, explaining how it can be possible and leaving that explanation to philosophy. One of the theoretical strategies that philosophy has sought to offer involves, as we shall examine further on, supposing that some of the constituent properties of an art work belong to the sphere of the invisible. In other words, they cannot be grasped through perception (Danto 1964) as they are not perceptible properties.

Document (1963) is a two-part work created by U.S. artist Robert Morris. A rather curious story lies behind the genesis of the piece. The larger part of the work is a rather infantile depiction of a previous work by Morris, entitled *Litanies* (1963). *Litanies* presents a series of keys, on each of which is inscribed a motto by Marcel Duchamp. *Litanies* was purchased by the architect Philip Johnson, who then failed to pay Morris the agreed sale price. That led the artist to create a second work, entitled *Document*, which for all intents and purposes is a document, as well as an actual work of art. To recap, *Document* is made up of two different elements: the citation of a work and a statement, i.e., a performative act. The citation is a stylized reproduction of the original work, that is, an actual representation of *Litanies*. The statement is instead a piece of writing placed alongside the representation, in which the artist withdraws from the first work, from *Litanies*, the work's identity as a work of art. *Document* says something about *Litanies*. Specifically, it says to the owner of that work that it is merely a material object that, from that moment onwards, has the same cultural and economic value that we would attribute to any steel object attached to a wooden base.

Morris's gesture was, for all intents and purposes, an act of withdrawing the identity of his former work through the production of a second work which essentially seeks to be a performative act, one that makes something happen in the world[7]—it is an object that excludes *Litanies* from the class of art works. Rules and agreements of social behaviour, Morris appears to be saying, are abided by because they are binding on those who enter and accept them voluntarily; if that does not happen, other rules, which govern that same behaviour, will be applied to restore justice to the situation. The artist does not deny his authorship of the work—the opposite of which is regularly pursued by archives and foundations whenever it is necessary to protect the name or legacy of an artist. Rather, Morris withdraws the aesthetic quality and content of the work, which means, in other words, that he denies the work means anything and denies that the object shows any aesthetic properties. Now, while the first denial (i.e., that the work means anything) falls at least partially within the powers of the artist, the denial of the work's aesthetic qualities, that the object has qualities that depend on human perception, is, quite frankly, more complicated. Morris's claim is that *Litanies* says nothing at all, or that it incorporates no meaning, and if it incorporates no aesthetic properties then *it is not a work of art*, but a common material object.[8] In practical terms, there is some doubt as to whether such a strategy can work; indeed *Litanies* is held by the Museum of Modern Art in New York and is considered for all intents and purposes a work of art. Of course, it could be argued that Morris subsequently withdrew his withdrawal, restoring the work of art to its original condition. The real point, however, from my perspective, is that through *Document*, Morris draws our attention to the meanings and dynamics of certain social practices, leading us to consider them more closely.

On the other hand, the artist could not simply have repudiated the authorship of *Litanies*, a work he himself had signed and thereby acknowledged, without violating another fundamental social rule, one which obliges us to make truthful statements and, consequently, to abide by those statements in every situation in which we can. As such, he came up with what was the rather bizarre idea of withdrawing the meaning and aesthetic qualities of the work, with a view to restoring the work to the status of mere object, at least from a symbolic point of view. The aesthetic qualities of the two works, however,

7 For an in-depth discussion of performatives see Austin (1962).

8 On these questions see Saw (1961, 18–29).

are something entirely secondary. They are of course present, but are of little importance given that both *Litanies* and *Document* could have been produced with completely different aspectual qualities. Since those qualities are not constituent properties, it is not clear what Morris wanted to withdraw. The blue of the background? The roundness of the key ring? Clearly, that is not the point. Rather, the point is to reflect on the type of performativeness that can be put into practice through art and, of equal importance, the types of analysis in which the arts can engage. Obviously they cannot be of the same depth as, say, an essay of sociology or philosophy, but they can nevertheless entail a certain degree of insight, for instance, as concerns the dynamics of how certain structures that make up social reality work and how emotions work.[9]

Different artist, different artistic genre. In 1964, Andy Warhol directed the motion picture *Empire*. As a cinema production, the film is rather curious, with a running time of 8 hours and 5 minutes, during which the camera remains focused and stationary on the Empire State Building. Over the entire length of the film, next to nothing happens. All we see are the changes in light, and the slight movement of a few objects in the distance. Overall, the scene seems to be completely static—a perception that is completely different to what we experience when watching a movie, so much so that it would be legitimate to observe that *Empire* is not really a 'motion picture' in the true sense of the term. In realty, as has been correctly observed (Danto and ebrary Inc. 2009), *Empire* is a film that by subtraction shows how motion is a property that is important but not necessary for defining works of art that belong to the specific class of 'cinema pieces'. A cinema piece is generally defined as a moving picture, yet *Empire* is a picture that is completely immobile for an extensive length of time, which lead us to ask what type of motion it is that film uses and, above all, whether a film can tell us anything without using what would appear to be a fundamental property of films, i.e., motion.

Let us look at another case. Banksy is a leading exponent of *street art*. That means he creates his works using media offered by streets, such as the walls of houses, rather than ordinary media, such as traditional canvases. More often than not, his media of choice consist of public and private buildings, of which he is not the owner. Like all street writers, Banksy draws and paints without asking permission from anybody, let alone the owners. Finally, 'Banksy' is a pseudonym. Nobody knows the true identity of the artist, who works at night so as not to be seen or recognised. Thus we have art works that belong to an artist whose public identity is unknown—nobody knows Banksy or who he really is. All we know of him are the traces he leaves by painting his murals. The

9 See, for example, Young (2001), Gaut and Lopes (2005), and Kieran and Lopes (2007).

works are produced on the walls of public and private buildings and conceived for those spaces. Ultimately, that means Banksy gifts them to the owners of those buildings, although they never asked for them. Recapping, we have an artist who is renowned although no identity—or traditional concept of authorship—can be linked to his pseudonym, and who paints his works on the walls of private homes or public buildings, which complicates not so much the matter of attributing the works—Banksy's touch is always clearly recognisable—but rather the matter of managing them, just as it complicates issues connected with the relationship between the works and the intentionality of the artist. In 2016, for example, a mural by Banksy was destroyed when the house on which it was painted in Cheltenham, Great Britain, was demolished. The action provoked an uproar among local residents, who had come to consider the mural a part of the neighbourhood itself, as though it were a public work of art. Yet Banksy's works do not observe the rules that regulate the production of public art. How are they to be protected and preserved when not only the specific intentions of the artist are unknown, but little to nothing is known about the genesis of the work—and when, moreover, no contract exists attesting the ownership of the work?

2.3 *Issues in Question*

Having explored the fortunes of a handful of works in their encounters with Customs and the courts, and the difficulties faced in cataloguing, interpreting, attributing, and protecting them, the point I wish to stress here is how contemporary art has raised a series of issues of great interest for philosophy, and how it has done so much more powerfully and directly than art before the turn of the twentieth century. At a first glance, we can classify those issues as follows:

1. *Ontological issues.* These issues encompass questions concerning the identity of a work, its classification, and, of course, its definition. In the twentieth century, the metaphysical question of the indiscernibility of art works from material objects came to the fore in philosophy as it enabled attention to be focused on the properties that works of art and mere artefacts do *not* share. The idea was that there must be something that distinguishes a simple bottle rack from a bottle rack that is a work of art. After Duchamp and his work, it began to be thought that that something was not necessarily a property to be sought in the sphere of the visible and perceptible.[10]

10 On these issues see Danto (1964; 1968; 1981; 1986; 1992), Dickie (1969; 1974), Carroll (2000), and Goldsmith (1983).

2. *Aesthetic issues*. These issues radically problematize the idea that beauty is a necessary property of works of art. In general, aspectual properties appear to be less important because artists make use of properties of a semantic nature, reflecting on how they are embodied and on the possibilities of their use. Such considerations also underscore the idea that art does not just 'say' things, but is also capable of producing effects in the world, thus it is capable of fulfilling a performative function of some sort.
3. *Issues connected with the sphere of judgement*. Aesthetic judgement and the judgement of taste concern fundamental issues of aesthetics and art criticism. Commonly, we think that works of art have an idiomatic identity which confers on them a value that is similarly idiomatic. Hence, classifying an object in the class of works of art, even if it does not necessarily mean classifying it more specifically as a masterpiece, implicitly implies accrediting the object with a judgement of value. Objects that we classify as works of art have some sort of value.
4. *Issues connected with the sphere of value*. That all suggests the need to rethink the idea of value connected with art, which clearly no longer depends, exclusively or predominantly, on it possessing or displaying particular technical skills required to produce aesthetic properties above all, especially beauty. Questions such as, What is it worth? Why is it of worth? What sort of worth does it have? are no longer obvious questions, for which common sense struggles to find a shared response. That arises above all because what I call the 'standard theory of value in art', to which we shall turn in the following pages, appears patently inadequate in accounting for the developments and changes that have emerged in the sphere of value as concerns works of art. All this, moreover, in a context in which the world of art has become a market of increasing complexity and sophistication, in which works of art are treated as stores of economic value.[11]
5. *Issues connected with the sphere of property*. As we mentioned earlier, then there are issues connected with property ownership, which depend appreciably on earlier metaphysical assumptions. For example, they depend on how we consider the relationship between a work of art and its maker and between a work of art and the viewer, and on how we categorize 'works of art'.
6. *Issues connected with the normative sphere*. Finally, there is the sphere of normativity, which in turn is deeply tied to the sphere of value. Does

11 On this issue see in particular Belting, Buddensieg, and Weibel (2013), Carrier and Pissarro (2013), Dimitrakaki and Lloyd (2015), Findlay (2012), Poli (1975; 2011), and Zarobell (2017).

some kind of normativity still exist in the contemporary arts? If it does, how is it organized and what forms has it taken?

Addressing the question of definition, that is, whether it is possible to identify at least the necessary conditions that make an object, or an action, a work of art, means reasoning about these issues in an effort to build theories that are as inclusive as possible and that attempt to explain the choices and directions taken by artists and, finally, illustrate the ontology of art works.[12]

3 Theories

Let us now look at how philosophy of art in the twentieth century responded, or attempted to respond, to the issues raised by contemporary works. The contributions that appear most significant include, more or less, five theoretical approaches: essentialism (versions one and two); functionalism; artefactualism; institutionalism; and historical contextualism.[13] Here we shall focus on the three approaches that most significantly marked the twentieth century and the philosophy of contemporary art, namely, essentialism (versions one and two), institutionalism, and, finally, historical contextualism. Each of these positions has generated theoretical developments that arrive, in some cases, at very different conclusions. Here we shall focus only on the most exemplary positions, in an effort to illustrate the problems they present and the solutions they offer.

12 For a careful and intelligent reconstruction of the questions concerning definition since the dawn of art history see Tatarkiewicz (1980). Tatarkiewicz proposes a genealogy of the concept of art. The earliest definition of which we have evidence dates back to Galen, who defined art as a set of rules: "*Ars est sistema preceptorum universalium, consentientium, ad unum eudemque finem tendentium.*" The underlying distinction, common to all practices shaping the idea that art was the application of a series of rules, was that between the physical arts and the rational arts. Despite there being many candidates, the arts were reduced to seven main types. It is notable how poetry was not initially considered an art, but rather a divinatory and religious practice. When the seven arts were finally identified, involving the exclusion of activities based on the sciences or on crafts, and the inclusion of poetry in the list, one of the fundamental criteria proved to be utility. As a result, in that first classification of the arts, both the visual arts and sculpture were considered of only marginal importance (Tatarkiewicz 1980, 11–15).

13 For a general overview see Andina (2013).

3.1 *Essentialism, Version One: The Transcendentalist Approach*

What I call the 'transcendentalist approach' can be exemplified, I believe, by the theoretical school of Hegel–Nietzsche–Heidegger, that is, the ideas developed by Georg Hegel, Friedrich Nietzsche, and Martin Heidegger with regard to the metaphysical questions posed by art. What we will find is that there is a common thread linking the thought of these three philosophers on art, a thread that consists of the idea that the domain of art is the expression of a dimension tied to the metaphysical sphere. Art, in short, is connected with the noumenon, in the sense that it is a sort of link between ordinary reality and that something—whatever it is—that transcends it. In that sense, art has to do with truth.

The point has been a particularly sensitive one ever since Kant, who in his first introduction to the *Critique of Judgement* distinguished between two different types of 'aesthetics' which, over the centuries, would lead to the development of radically different ways of understanding art. The first conception of aesthetics relates to sensibility and concerns, specifically, the object—the greenness of a field, the fragrance of a flower, the pinkness of the sky at dusk. It concerns what we usually classify as aesthetic properties. The second conception concerns the fact that the perception of such objects, connoted by an aesthetic dimension, is tied to judgement, a judgement which, in these terms, does not produce knowledge but a feeling of agreeableness or disagreeableness. These two different ways of understanding aesthetics produced a deep divide in the philosophy of art over the idea of whether art has to do with truth or not. Hegel, Nietzsche, and Heidegger, to remain focused on the more prominent positions in the field, believed that it did, hence their theories should be read in the light of their relative metaphysics. All three of them were essentialists, which means they believed that what we call art has an essence that is not the outcome of an act of stipulation, and they were guided by the conviction, which is perhaps the most significant aspect of their thought, that art, however narrowly imperfectly, reveals essential aspects of reality. Alongside this form of essentialism, however, is another of a different kind, which does not link art to the revelation of being.

3.1.1 Georg Wilhelm Hegel: Art as Incorporation of Spirit

Hegel's published thoughts on art are found in paragraphs 556–563 of the *Encyclopaedia* (1830). Alongside other published workers, scholars also refer to his *Aesthetics*, a text published by a student of Hegel's, Heinrich Gustav Hotho, based on Hegel's manuscripts and a series of lecture transcripts. Hegel anticipated an approach that would later be developed in different ways by Nietzsche and Heidegger, by establishing a clear dependency between art and truth in its transcendental dimension. Thus, preliminarily, we can say that art, for Hegel, is dependent on being, and being has to do with a certain acceptation of truth. But let us proceed one step at a time, and start by clarifying how Hegel understands, in this context, truth. Here, truth is not conformity. Rather, truth is connected with the formation of being, or, to use the Hegelian term, the spirit. Being, for Hegel, is self-determining reason, or idea. Self-determination, however, is not confined exclusively to the logical sphere; rather, it takes form through its embodiment in nature. Nature follows rules that belong to the idea at the logical level. However, while all of nature responds to rational principles, only life is self-determining, and it is only human life that becomes self-conscious. Understood that way, human beings are not the causal outcome of nature, but rather its articulation at a fuller and higher level, the most complete expression of the possibility of self-determination. In the objective spirit, Hegel identifies the institutions that best enable the self-determination of the spirit in the law, the family, society, and the state. The spirit attains its fullest form of understanding in the absolute spirit. That understanding is articulated specifically in three forms, in art, religion, and philosophy, each of which, notoriously, incorporates the truth of the former. Religion and philosophy are two determinations in which the self-understanding of the spirit is attained in abstract terms. Of the two, philosophy, as it is more abstract, enables a more perfect understanding of the spirit than religion, while they both articulate forms of self-understanding of the spirit that are more perfect than what is possible through art, again because they are more abstract. Nevertheless, in this framework, Hegel stresses how the self-understanding of the spirit needs not only concepts, as in religion and in philosophy, but also images for its articulation. Hence the necessity of art. Thus, even art is a form of self-understanding of the spirit, a form embodied in matter, in images, and in objects specifically created for the purpose. Beauty is, therefore, the self-understanding of the spirit rendered in sensible form. Two implications derive from that conclusion. The first is that art and beauty are two concepts that are necessarily linked to each other. The second is that art serves no mimetic purpose. Rather, its purpose is to enable the extrinsic expression of the spirit in sensible form—a form that is less perfect than the rational but nevertheless necessary. Hegel refers to three forms of art that each constitute embodiments that are not just different but show different levels of development—romantic art, classical art, and symbolic art. While classical art shows full maturity, romantic art shows a level of immaturity that will eventually disappear, whereas symbolic art is still fundamentally immature. Here, the concept of 'immaturity' obviously has to do with the expression of the spirit, its degree and tangibility.

This is not, however, the time and place to examine in detail Hegel's aesthetics. What interests us, besides his general framework and how art is specifically tied to a precise conception of truth, is Hegel's treatment of symbols, which, as we shall see, would undergo rather interesting developments in later philosophy of art. The symbol is distinguished by the particular connection it holds with the thing it symbolizes. To put it in other words, the symbol, as opposed to what occurs with conventional signs, includes in its structure a direct reference to the thing it symbolizes. The rabbit for instance, is considered a symbol of fertility, therefore in appropriate contexts a representation of a rabbit induces us to connect the thing symbolized with the idea of fertility. Such an association is not a random one, but is made precisely because rabbits are considered fertile animals, so there exists a direct connection between the symbol and the thing it symbolizes, between the symbol and ordinary reality. On the other hand, it should be observed that the symbol as such cannot be reduced to the symbolic meaning manifested. In other words, there is a surplus of meaning that goes beyond the manifest symbolic meaning. Rabbits do not just symbolize fertility. In the universe of meanings of the vegetarian world, for instance, the rabbit symbolizes an animal to be defended and refers to a certain ethical orientation. Similarly, the representation of a rabbit will show features, for instance stylistic features, that belong to the representation and not to a rabbit in flesh and blood. Furthermore, just like art can, the symbol can offer space for a potentially vast stratification of meanings. The White Rabbit, for instance, is a character invented by the pen of Lewis Carroll, which first appeared in 1862 in *Alice's Adventures Under Ground*, and then in 1965 in *Alice's Adventures in Wonderland*. All we know of the White Rabbit are the features Carroll gives the character in describing its behaviour. The White Rabbit is the Queen of Heart's herald, who opens processions by announcing the court and is present at the Knave of Heart's trial. The character is a rather curious rabbit, as imagined by Carroll—it walks on two feet, has pink eyes, and wears a funny waistcoat in which it carries a pocket watch. Rather than drawing on rabbit features, the White Rabbit looks more like a grumpy old man who is chiefly absorbed by his own problems and could not care less about anything else. What is more, he agonizes over the passing of time, seeing as all he does is lament how late it is. The White Rabbit refers back to a series of symbolic universes that intersect, drawing on the human world at times, on the animal world at others, to create a blend of both. Thus the White Rabbit is a symbol that encompasses a multitude of semantic stratifications and refers to different 'worlds'—the human world, the animal world, and the worlds of fiction. The peculiar structure of symbols (which depends on ordinary reality, may refer to fictional worlds, and often concerns art) makes them privileged objects for the understanding of art, independently of Hegel's specific perspective. The issues they raise are preliminary to any understanding of art in general and, as we shall see, of contemporary art in particular. But let us focus on Hegel's idea that art in some way has to do with the determining of the spirit, in a process which substantially coincides with the determining of truth. As we shall see in the next section, it was an idea that both Nietzsche and Heidegger did not dislike at all.

3.1.2 Friedrich Nietzsche: Art as Metaphysical Condition

Nietzsche, in particular, held that art is the only metaphysics possible (Nietzsche 1927). The metaphysics in Nietzsche's later philosophy is much more sophisticated than the sketch found in his early writings and transcends the dimension of art. His early thoughts on metaphysics are nevertheless of particular interest. Drawing on certain elements found in Schopenhauer (2010), Nietzsche argues that art is a kind of open space for the creation of individual identity, a poietic space in which the fundamental instincts identifying nature in general, and human nature in particular, can be modelled and shaped. It is a formative activity, which Nietzsche conceives as transfigurative and which takes place through a *medium*, which is both the vehicle and the substance of the process. The concept of *medium* is fundamental for philosophies of contemporary art and Nietzsche takes a very interesting approach to retracing the different ways that the medium is transformed in art, especially as regards the performing arts. First of all, he looks at the transformations of the actor in classical tragedy. The origin of tragedy lies in that subtle space that separates the ordinary world—the world of logical thought and the rational dimension—from the pre-logical world, a dimension in which, as Nietzsche imagined it, pure forces of nature live side by side in their spontaneous, unorganized dimension. It is from that imaginative and symbolic reservoir that art takes shape and organizes its meanings through the creation of works. And it does so primarily by refining a conceptual tool that is also key to accessing the world, namely representation, or the awareness of those who enjoy and create art that the medium is not the thing, but a representation of the thing. The medium is, therefore, the tool enabling reference to the thing. In the case of classical tragedy, so dear to Nietzsche, the logical step is that from the figure of the person who, in a religious procession, is understood to be presenting a divinity, lending his body for its presentation to those gathered in the procession, to the figure of the actor, who, in contrast, simply represents the transcendental sphere (Nietzsche 2008, 50ff). The passage from the *is* that is the simple presentation of the thing to the *is* that is its representation effectuates the passage from the religious sphere to that of art—a key passage in the evolution of individual practices as well as social practices.

Although Nietzsche is perfectly convinced that the heuristic potential of human beings, as well as of the more gifted animals in that sense, is largely limited by their physical and perceptive conformation, nevertheless, as concerns art, and in *The Birth of Tragedy* at least, he appears to leave room for the idea that art is the practice that lies in the space separating the subject from the world, in all its various dimensions. Art erupts from nature, without the need for mediation, as a world of dream images through Apollonian forces, and as vitalistic reality through Dionysian forces. Such states are intrinsically artistic, or, in Nietzsche's terms, propaedeutic to creation, with regard to which the artist is an imitator. Art, for Nietzsche in *The Birth of Tragedy*, is humanity's only authentic chance for salvation. The Greeks, after having suffered the terrible cruelty of nature, managed to redeem themselves through the sentiment of joyful power that comes with cosmic unity, experienced through the dance of the satyr chorus. Art for the Greeks was an escape from the risk of passive nihilism, which is primarily the negation of the will, and it continues to be the deepest of consolations, the greatest stimulus for life that life has ever known. Only art is able to transform the sentiment of refusing life into representations that humans can live with.[14] In that way, while art provides a bridge between the human dimension and the most profound aspects of nature, it is also a means enabling human beings to give shape to the shapeless chaos of nature, and to do so without undermining the essence of life. In that sense, art for Nietzsche is an essential means of enabling the individual to keep the energy that forms life intact, while opening up the possibility of sustaining it at the same time.

As an aside, it is worth stressing how Nietzsche addressed the general question of the problem of art first, before turning to works of art. In other words, the point for Nietzsche was not to answer the question, what is a work of art? Rather, from a philosophical perspective at least, he uses his considerations on works of art—*The Birth of Tragedy*, in fact, addresses the rather circumscribed question of how it is possible that classical tragedy died by its own hand—to respond to the general question posed by art, which is, substantially, what is art and what is its purpose? From the Nietzschean perspective, the purpose of art is to render life fulfilling and sustainable, through instantiations of various kinds. Therefore, art—whatever it is and however we want to define it—serves to make a worthy life possible, which means, in Nietzsche's terms, self-awareness and, hence, courage. Nietzsche's answer to why classical tragedy, the most perfect form of art, should have suddenly died, moreover by its own hand, is interesting because it concerns, first and foremost, the value judgement that

14 See Nietzsche (2008).

Euripides gave of life. In Euripides's view, life is meaningful if it is fully ushered back to the dimension of the *logos*. Consequently, art, as a means of life, must seek to usher the plurality of instincts that characterize it back to a single dimension, that of logic. Thus Euripides, working within the framework of Socratic teachings, systematically worked to overthrow the Apollonian–Dionysian dichotomy to the advantage of Apollo and calculating reason. The result of his efforts was that tragic art became completely transparent, logical, and consistent. In short, it was reduced to philosophy, or rather, it became very similar to philosophy based fundamentally on *logos*. For Nietzsche, however, art embraces a whole range of instincts that simply cannot be dismissed or completely circumscribed. Thus it would avenge itself on philosophy and on what would later emerge as a millenarian effort to depose it, through the dialectical form that Plato adopted for his dialogues. The dialogues, in fact, are "suspended between narrative, lyric, and drama, between prose and poetry" (Nietzsche 2008, 77); they are the concrete exemplification of the contamination between art and philosophy that Euripides had sought to overthrow, by reducing art to philosophy. Which is to say that art cannot be deposed by philosophy—something aspired to as much by Plato as by Hegel—quite simply because it is something other to philosophy, represented by a range of different instincts and serving a different purpose in the relationship between humanity and the world. In spite of its rationalist premises, Plato's philosophy is unable to articulate what it means except through the language of poetry. Thus, from the enemy of rationality as it was presented in the *Ion*, art becomes a handmaid without which philosophy cannot entirely fulfil its task. Although philosophy, in the writings of Plato, manifestly shows its need for art, at the same time it seeks to subordinate art to its purposes and renders it a vicarious philosophy with moral and pedagogic ends.

In *The Birth of Tragedy* (1872), Nietzsche confers on art, exemplarily on classical tragedy, the function of describing two fundamental instincts that identify the essence of nature. In classical tragedy, the Apollonian and Dionysian spirits, through a series of technical expedients, are reconciled perfectly. Art is once again the appropriate medium not only to articulate such reconciliation, but to actually constitute it. It will not have been overlooked that one of the few foundations of Nietzsche's metaphysics is, specifically, nature, which thus discloses its deeper essence, and in doing so constitutes it. That is, in a way, the only truth that is welcomed somehow within Nietzsche's system. If what nature is is true, and nature is made up of the composition of elements that form it, then the only truth is that expressed in artistic, or creative, form by nature itself. There is no question, therefore, of defining art in a strict sense. Just as Hegel did, when Nietzsche refers to art, he is substantially referring to the sphere of truth, in the only understanding of it that he considers accessible to human beings.

3.1.3 Martin Heidegger: Truth in Art

In Nietzsche's framework, therefore, art is a means of understanding and shaping life. Art works are the space that makes that possible, while artists embody the form of life tasked with making such mediation possible. Heidegger's system of thought, although literally very different to Nietzsche's, is prompted by much the same intuition, which is that to understand art, we need to embrace an idea that encompasses two approaches. The first involves inquiry into art as a class; the second involves inquiry into art works. The first cannot prescind from the second, as is paradigmatically demonstrated by Martin Heidegger in his essay entitled *The Origin of the Work of Art* (1950). Heidegger's essay focuses on the question posed by art and, taking an approach that was adopted also by Nietzsche, draws the question of art back into the more complex framework of a systematic speculation on Being and on the distinction between beings and Being (Heidegger 2008, 5ff).[15] The question of Being in the horizon opened by Heidegger is a question of "fundamental ontology". On the one hand, it grounds all other ontologies; on the other, it itself is grounded in existence as a particular way of being of Being-here. *Fundamentalontologie*, therefore, takes as its starting point Being-here and consists of "laying bare the horizon for an Interpretation of the meaning of Being in general" (Heidegger 1967, 36).

Heidegger scholars identify the *Kehre*, or the turn from the ontology formulated in *Being and Time*, in the introduction of temporality in the fundamental ontology proposed by Heidegger. Temporality is a key element for understanding questions relating to art, and the German term that Heidegger uses is "*Ereignis*", or event. In Heidegger's terminology, the concept of 'event' takes on a very specific meaning. It is not an event in the common meaning of the term as something that happens; rather, Heidegger develops a conception of the term that links event to truth. To understand truth, it is necessary to understand the dynamics of concealment and unconcealment. In that sense, event becomes the coming into view of entities, which, however, neither appear nor manifest themselves. The manifestation of entities is an event that involves the human being to whom the entity appears—that is how human beings participate in the dynamics of truth. Entities need human beings to manifest themselves, while human beings are a property of the entities. Entities and human beings are linked by a relationship that constitutes them within the scope

15 For a discussion of the meaning of Heidegger's interest in art see Pöggeler (1987) and Harries (2009).

of the relationship that links them. In his *Contributions to Philosophy* (2012), Heidegger defines the *Ereignis* at several points as "hesitant denial" and "self-withholding", as in manifesting entities, the event conceals itself and grounds by withdrawing. Thus the question of ground returns with insistence and, far from being understood in a metaphysical sense (and hence as substance, substrate, and, ultimately, as being), it is identified by Heidegger as *Ab-grund*. Thus the ground is an abyss, a ground without a ground. Nevertheless, it is not the absence of ground (*Un-grund*), but rather a back-ground (*Ur-grund*, i.e., original ground). The abyssal ground is an emptiness understood as fullness, which supports what comes out in the Open (where the Open is the horizon of manifestation of entities)—it is as empty as can be to the extent that it is an abyss, but at the same time it is as full as can be, in the sense that it is the opening of all possibilities. The *Ab-grund* (abyss) is still a *Grund* (ground), albeit in its own peculiar way, as it grounds by withdrawing, and it does so for intrinsic and constitutive reasons. If the ground came to view as ground, coming out into the Open in the same way beings do, it would lose its grounding character and be reduced to a grounded being. If Being cannot, therefore, be reduced to beings (since it is not a being and it is not ground or metaphysical cause of beings), then it is the event of becoming present to beings. In that sense, the essence of beings is constitutively dynamic—it is not a static *essentia* but *Wesen*, a word that is originally an infinite verb, and not a noun. It is the disclosing of their Being, and this process is given or consists in the "grounding by withdrawing" of the *Ereignis* as an *Ab-grund*. All this gives us an ontology that is essentially dynamic, in which everything has always been in motion and nothing is static.

That is the metaphysical framework in which Heidegger's theory of art needs to be framed. The most significant elements of that theory are found in the essays *The Origin of the Work of Art* and *The Age of the World Picture*, both of which were published in the collection of works *Holzwege* (1950), now published in English as *Off the Beaten Track* (2002). What interests Heidegger to begin with is not the question of the ontology of art, but rather, in a move reminiscent of Nietzsche's, the question of its origin. Where does art come from? Heidegger's answer from the very start of the essay is: from the relationship linking art to truth.

Far from being tied to reality by a mimetic relationship, as theorized by Plato (1993), who notoriously considered works of art to be imperfect copies of a degraded nature of things, Heidegger decides to analyse the ontological specificity of works by inquiring into what distinguishes them from mere things. Why is it that an art work, which is certainly a thing, in the sense that in most cases it is a physical object, does not reduce to a mere thing? And why can it not be reduced to a mere thing when it is interpreted?

> If we regard works in their pristine reality and do not deceive ourselves, the following becomes evident: works are as naturally present [*Vorhandenheit*] as things. The picture hangs on the wall like a hunting weapon or a hat. [...] Works are shipped like coal from the Ruhr or logs from the Black Forest. [...] Every work has this thingly character [*dinghaft*].
>
> HEIDEGGER 2002, 2–3

It is clear that Heidegger could hardly have imagined that it would not be long before philosophers would be faced not only with *Bottle Racks* and *Bicycle Wheels* making their way into museums and claiming the same legitimacy to do so as the works of Giotto and Rafael, but even works lacking any physical consistency at all, but declared to be art by conceptual artists. In those years (the essay was written in 1927), one of the key aspects that art was beginning to show, if we think, for example, of ready-mades, was that works were increasingly indistinguishable from ordinary objects. And on a closer look, if we separate Heidegger's thoughts from his general metaphysical system, it is quite simple to see how his starting question about art, if circumscribed at least to the matter of works, is the same that Arthur Danto would later ask from another perspective.

Adopting what in many ways is a classical style of reasoning, Heidegger chooses to present various theories that offer an answer before setting out his own theory. He outlines three solutions to the question of the origin of art, which he considers canonical. The first defines a thing as the substance (ὑποκείμενον) of accidents (συμβεβηκότα); the second characterises a things as αἰσθητόν (meaning a unity, or agglomerate, of a multiplicity of sensory data). The third theory is presented by Heidegger as the one that has had the biggest and most characteristic influence, for which he describes it as "the conceptual scheme deployed in the greatest variety of ways by all art theory and aesthetics" (Heidegger 2002, 9). It is the theory that describes a work of art as the unity of matter (ὕλη) and form (μορφή). But according to Heidegger, what we can define as the unity of matter and form is not the work, but the medium, which occupies an ontologically mid-way position between a mere thing and a work of art. The main property of the medium, however, is it serviceability, which is a property that cannot be attributed to an art work in its capacity as an art work. In other words, if there is one property that certainly cannot identify a work of art, it is serviceability. Art works are not created to serve a functional purpose the way traditional implements are. It would be absurd to claim that painters paint to conceal the imperfections of a wall. Similarly, it can hardly be true that they do so to flatter their patrons, despite the fact that for centuries patronage was an important component of artists' work. Art, for Heidegger, serves a different purpose, and to understand it we need to go back to the question of its origin.

The theoretical strategy adopted by Heidegger consists of an analysis of the functions of the medium, so as to distinguish it analytically from the work of art. Thus he focuses on a specific work of art, a painting by Van Gogh that portrays a pair of shoes.[16] Heidegger interprets the pair of shoes as belonging to a peasant. What difference is there between a pair of shoes, i.e., the means we traditionally use to protect our feet and move around comfortably, and the portrayal of a pair of shoes, like the many examples offered by Van Gogh? Essentially, the latter is of a superior order to the former, or rather, they each have a different origin and different purpose. Van Gogh did not paint shoes so as to protect his feet in some way, or as designs for somebody else to produce the shoes physically. Rather, what is happening is that shoes disclose something about the world which Van Gogh chose to convey to us. "The artwork let us know what the shoes, in truth, are. [...] what comes to explicit appearance first and only through the work is the equipmental being of the equipment" (Heidegger 2002, 15–16). Van Gogh's painting is thus "the disclosure of what the equipment, the pair of peasant shoes, in truth *is*. This being steps forward into the unconcealment of its being (*Un-verborgenheit*)" (Heidegger 2002, 16). It is undoubtedly true that shoes are made for walking, in the sense that their primary purpose is to serve as equipment designed to enable the wearer to move. Yet, if we take a closer look and pay attention not only to their purpose, but observe the complex web of references that emerges from them, we can understand something more about the world to which the shoes, as equipment, belong.[17] A work of art is the special object that makes that kind of experience possible, an experience that is eminently gnosiological since, as Heidegger conceives it, it enables us to attain a more complete understanding of the being depicted in the work and, ultimately, the being in general:

> In the work, when there is a disclosure of the being as what and how it is, there is a happening of truth at work. In the work of art, the truth of the being has set itself to work. [...] art is truth's setting-itself-to-work.
>
> HEIDEGGER 2002, 16

---

16 Van Gogh, *A Pair of Shoes* (1886, oil on canvas, 37.5 × 45.5cm, Amsterdam, Van Gogh Museum).

17 On the question of the centrality of attention for aesthetic experience see Nanay (2016).

Heidegger's position is a radical one. The work of art does not just capture something that is there, traits of the world that come to light in the work, but appears as the event that makes it possible for the truth of the being shown in the work to emerge. The truth of the work is disclosed in the work, and that dynamic is event, which has the peculiarity of not just unconcealing, but also concealing. The struggle between concealment and unconcealment (which is the very essence of truth) eminently unfolds in the work of art thanks to its peculiar constitution. Heidegger, in fact, identifies two principal characteristics of the work's being-a-work. On the one hand, it displays a World (*Welt*) on the other it brings forth the Earth (*Erde*). World is defined by Heidegger as a principle of openness and light, which is established by the work of art—it is in that sense (and not in a museum sense) that the work displays a World. Earth, instead, withdraws; it is a principle that is closed, obscure and impenetrable, yet, as Heidegger effectively shows with the example of the Greek temple, it is the ground that sets up the world and supports it. The two principles are reciprocal. The work of art is the embodiment of that struggle, and it is by virtue of its special role that art holds a privileged relationship to truth.

Thus, for Heidegger, the work of art has a privileged relationship to truth, which, from a general theoretical point of view, is not at all obvious. We shall return to this point more fully. In a system such as Heidegger's, in which the work assumes a foundational role, the origin of art—the question which initiates Heidegger's inquiry—cannot be anything else but art itself. Art is the setting-to-work of truth because it originates truth itself. Hence truth becomes both that which is set to work and that which sets to work, taking us back into the vortex of the hermeneutic circle which Heidegger discusses in the Introduction to *Being and Time*. The work of art is, therefore, the device that enables truth to emerge from its concealment and become present in the work, which happens, as Heidegger conceives it, without the material structure of the work, its body, having any particular importance. That is also why the German philosopher separates in practice the work of art from both the history of art and the history of effects, in relation, at least, to the interpretation and construal of works.

A celebrated critique of Heidegger's essay from the artworld, and hence not from a philosophical perspective, was advanced by the art critic Meyer Schapiro (1968). Schapiro effectively demonstrated the substantial lack of concern shown by Heidegger for elementary notions of philology, of the history of the work, and of art history itself, by noting how it was indifferent for Heidegger's inquiry to specify which of the various depictions of shoes painted by Van Gogh was being treated by the philosophical analysis, which nevertheless revolves around an interpretation of the work. We know that Van Gogh produced eight paintings of shoes. Schapiro demonstrated how the pair of shoes in the painting analysed by Heidegger were not the shoes of a peasant, as the German philosopher presumed, but rather the painter's own pair of boots. Hence, if the work gives any insight into a world, it was Van Gogh's world and not the world of a random peasant. Shapiro was trenchant in his conclusion:

> Alas for him, the philosopher has indeed deceived himself. He has retained from his encounter with van Gogh's canvas a moving set of associations with peasants and the soil, which are not sustained by the picture itself. They are grounded rather in his own social outlook with its heavy pathos of the primordial and earthy. He has indeed 'imagined everything and projected it into the painting.' He has experienced both too little and too much in his contact with the work.
>
> SCHAPIRO 1968, 206

The point here is not simply to expose a certain sloppiness in Heidegger's treatment of the details constituting the work posited at the centre of his analysis. Rather, it is to point out how the theoretical approach contemplated by the German philosopher, which in many ways is similar, in its general metaphysical framework at least, to Nietzsche's approach, not only completely sacrifices the interpretation of the work to philosophy, but shows how philosophy tends to empty art of meaning to adapt it to its purposes. Thus Heidegger produces a bad interpretation, or an interpretation that does not take into account the work's own characteristics (both formal and historical), which leads us to presume that the philosophy that underpins his bad interpretation is as shaky as the interpretation it produces. Heidegger treats the work of art as a device serving the disclosure of truth, which leads us to wonder why he chose art when art as such did not ultimately interest him—the same purpose of concealing and unconcealing truth could have been attributed, for example, to history. The work as such therefore becomes the site for the disclosure of a truth that the work itself produces, in a process that pivots around truth, not art. The impression is that art is somehow accidental to it all. Thus Heidegger paradoxically ends up treating art as a device, bringing works back down to the level of mere things.

I believe it is no coincidence that Nietzsche fell afoul of a similar error and that, ultimately, Heidegger simply proposed a variation of what we shall call the 'Nietzschean fallacy', a fallacy that implies a form of disenfranchisement of art.

3.2 *Essentialism, Version Two: What Art Is*

Alongside the transcendental version of essentialism, which seeks to interpret art as a means for truth to emerge, there is a second form of essentialism, which considers art to be independent and separate from truth. Indeed, as we shall see, it goes even further by considering art to be the sphere *par excellence* in which it makes no sense at all to pose the question of truth, and instead privileges the idea that inquiring into the ontology of art means inquiring into the necessary properties that are constituent of art. Such a position was developed in a number of paradigmatic ways by the American philosopher Arthur C. Danto,[18] who for good reason explicitly associated his philosophy of art with Hegel's. In reality, the two positions can probably be distinguished more convincingly than Danto himself was inclined to do. It is true that Danto takes from Hegel the idea that art embodies meaning to produce a secular version of the Hegelian concept of art as expression of spirit. However, contrary to Hegel, he also holds that art need not preoccupy itself, except in a very specific understanding of the concept, with the domain of truth. But let us put first things first.

Danto himself was no aesthetician. An analytic philosopher, he began his career studying philosophy of history (1965), epistemology (1968b), and philosophy of action (1973). His first foray into the philosophy of art came in what in many ways would become a seminal work, a paper entitled "The Artworld" (1964). In the paper, Danto lay the groundwork for the development of his essentialist theory of art, including a number of ideas that would be taken up independently and used in an original way, which Danto himself did not endorse, by institutional theories of art. Danto's work takes an observation as its starting point (the profound change being witnessed in artistic practice) and lays the groundwork for a new framework of inquiry in philosophy of art. From a methodological perspective, Danto's treatment of the question falls within the sphere of descriptive metaphysics. *If* the artworld (a specific entity which Danto posits in his eponymous article) and artists, in particular, produce works that seem eccentric when compared to the canon of art handed down by history, *then* philosophy is required to account for transformations in art from the point of view of the ontology of works and for transformations in the concept itself. In many ways, "The Artworld" provides the framework for a project that Danto would address in all its complexity only later in what would be his masterpiece in philosophy of art, namely, *The Transfiguration of the Commonplace*

18 For a comprehensive overview of Danto's philosophy, and in particular his philosophy of art, see Andina (2011), Auxier and Hahn (2013), and Rollins (2012).

(1981), a work that poses the ontological question of art in a more comprehensive perspective.

Starting from the observation of contemporary works of art, in "The Artworld" Danto essentially addresses the questions raised by (i) the inability of the imitation theory of art (also known as the mimetic theory of art)[19] to account for changes witnessed in contemporary art; (ii) the specificity of artistic representation; (iii) the ontological distinction between works and mere things;[20] (iv) two indiscernible objects that are nevertheless different in some way from an ontological point of view; or (v) the matter of two works that are apparently indiscernible from the point of view of their phenomenal properties, yet different from the point of view of their artistic classification; and (vi) the introduction of the concept of the artworld. Thus, "The Artworld" offers a complete framework of inquiry into the philosophy of art to account for to the changes witnessed in twentieth-century art. Danto would go on to fill out that framework in following works, starting with his masterpiece *The Transfiguration of the Commonplace* (1981). In that work, Danto tackles a fundamental goal, which is to outline a definition (in terms of necessary and sufficient conditions) of the concept of art work. Over the years and in the works that followed (1984; 1986; 1987; 1997), Danto reformulated that goal by stating he would work exclusively on the identification of necessary conditions.

Let us now look more closely at a brief reconstruction of Danto's philosophy of art, starting from the theoretical framework developed in "The Artworld".

3.2.1 Imitation and Representation

Danto begins with the imitation theory of art (IT), which, in its Platonic formulation, states that works of art, from an ontological point of view, are things that are copies of other things. So, if the real world is made up of things that are copies of things deemed of greater perfection, that is, Ideas, works of art are copies of copies, or copies of objects that furnish the world. Thus, a pictorial depiction of a bed is a copy of a thing we call 'bed'. The imitation theory thus propounds an explanation of both the ontology of works of art (i.e., it answers the question 'what?') and the value of art. As mere copies, however, works have very little value—as is exactly the case with copies, as opposed to

19 The theory was first introduced, in its initial formulation, by Plato. For a modern rendering of the theory see Batteux (1746). For a detailed discussion of the differences in the imitation theories offered by Plato and Aristotle see Abrams (1953, 8ff.).

20 It is important to remember that we can find in literature positions claiming there is no actual (ontological) difference between art and 'mere' things. See, as an example, Amie Thomasson (2005).

originals. Danto raises two points with regard to the mimetic theory. The first concerns the failure of the theory to explain works of art from the twentieth century. If we assume that a good theory should explain a certain domain of things as exhaustively and inclusively as possible, then we can only conclude that IT does not offer a satisfactory explanation to account for some of the art works that began to appear in the twentieth century. It follows that IT, in the formulation eminently held by Plato (1993, book X), needs to be reviewed, if not completely abandoned.

Danto offers an alternative theory which takes a more radical position. From a theoretical perspective, the fundamental weakness of IT lies in a radical misunderstanding of the nature of art. According to IT, art is essentially imitation of the real world. Danto propounds a completely different theory and argues that art does not imitate anything; rather it represents something, often the real world. Representation and imitation are two radically different things, even though the difference is not always so limpidly rendered in everyday language. In *The Transfiguration of the Commonplace* (1981, 25ff), Danto concurs with Nietzsche in proposing the idea that the origin of representation, considering the matter through the lens of the genealogist, lies in the process of presenting divinities in religious processions. It is in that context that we can begin to see the transformation of the copula, of the 'is', which gradually enables the passage of the verb 'to be' from one which expresses identity to one which expresses reference. To say that a broomstick, as playfully ridden by a child, is a horse is not equivalent to identifying the broomstick with a horse. Rather, it means asserting that the broomstick is traditionally associated with certain properties that we associate with horses. Which in turn does not mean that broomsticks are horses, or that broomsticks share all or even a majority of the properties that define horses. Rather, it means that something—its shape, perhaps, or the fact that it can be easily ridden, if only as a game—leads us to invent games in which we associate it with horses. That is why the structure of any representation is so interesting for art, because through representation we can convey meanings that are completely, or partly, extraneous to the material media that convey them. The relationship between the medium and the meaning conveyed by the medium can be either completely extrinsic and stipulative (as in cases where the phoneme 'home' is associated with the grapheme 'h o m e') or, vice versa, there can be some sort of correspondence between the properties of the medium and the properties belonging to the represented objected that we choose to use for the purposes of representation.

Hence, it is evident that representation does not imply a correspondence between the properties of the represented object and those of the medium, i.e., that which we use to represent what we want to represent. Furthermore, the properties of representation (suppose the broomstick-horse) are precisely properties that belong to the representation and not to what we represent. In this regard, Danto distinguishes two types of representation. One is the representation of reality, which is required to satisfy a truth condition in relation to the thing represented. The other is artistic representation, which is never required to satisfy such a condition. In other words, if I have to represent a house or, at a more complex level, a historical fact, I am obviously required to consider the conditions that link my representation to the object represented and, undoubtedly in very different ways in the two cases, to the world. The house, just like the French Revolution, are part of the real world, albeit in very different ways, taking the concept in the broadest of possible acceptations. On the contrary, the representation of a winged horse, of Sherlock Holmes, or of Mona Lisa belong, for Danto, to a particular sphere that has to do with the fictional world. Representations concerning the fictional world in general, and the art world in particular, possess specific characteristics, the inquiry into which is the domain of the philosophy of art. And their primary characteristic is that they have no necessary relationship to truth. In the exact moment in which that fact was understood, which was precisely when, in Ancient Greece, it was realized that in religious processions the divinity did not appear on stage directly, but was instead conveyed by an actor whose face served as a medium to represent the divinity, we have the passage from mimesis[21] to representation. And it was essentially at that exact moment that the ontological space of art was opened up. Artistic representation possesses, for Danto, three key characteristics: a) it is always about something (*aboutness*); b) its aboutness is always identified by a style; and, finally, (c) it is a particular kind of representation that normally possesses a metaphorical structure, or a structure in which a term is substituted for another and the two are linked by their partial semantic overlap. It is obvious that by its very structural nature, metaphor leaves much more space for interpretation, while at the same time weakening the logical and rational connotations that constitute the object. It follows that interpretation lends itself better to understanding art than logical thought does.

3.2.2 Works and Mere Things

What motivated a profound reconsideration of the philosophy of contemporary art was the ready-made art of the twentieth century, which intentionally narrowed, to the point of eliminating, the distance between works and mere

21 In reality, the idea of art as mimesis, or as the reproduction of reality rather than its representation, has persisted at length outside of philosophy; see, for example, Leonardo et al. (1651, frg. 411).

things. In a certain sense, and this was very much true up until the turn of the twentieth century, when confronted with art we are confronted with things, or physical objects, that have the distinctive trait of having an artefactual quality, a quality that is often extremely refined. On the other hand, however, with the introduction of ready-mades in the world of art, the distinction between works and mere things became increasingly faint, to the point that it is no longer possible, apparently at least, to distinguish the two classes of objects, in the sense that mere things have become works of art, as in the case of *Fountain* and other ready-mades by Marcel Duchamp. That diminishment of the aura of art is a process identified by Walter Benjamin (1963), who, more or less in those same years, stressed how works of art had lost their aura due to the powerful means of mechanical reproduction. That is, they had lost, or risked losing, that 'something' which distinguishes works from mere things. The fact that at a certain point it became possible to reproduce a work of art an infinite number of times, more or less perfectly and preserving all its quality, and produce, ultimately, indiscernible objects, raised the risk of the work losing its value, and that seemed true, above all, for works of visual art. Thus we have two essential points: the fact that technical progress enables the mass production of things that formerly were unique, as they could not be reproduced without the hand of the artist; and the fact that mere things can aspire, at the request of the artist, to have a different ontological status through their introduction in museums as works of art.

The observation of how artists had decided to make use of mere things to produce their works, without significantly altering the properties of the objects they use to create their art, led Danto to call on philosophy to investigate whether things were really as they seemed and whether, in the case of works such as ready-mades, the work coincides with the mere thing. For if it does, then on what basis can an ontological distinction be made? The argument Danto constructs offers an insightful response to the question of the ontology of works of art. It is based on the idea that a work of art is not constituted by the physical properties alone of the object. Of course, such properties are essential, but they are not all that makes up the work, which instead is given also by other properties of a relational and contextual nature. Together they are, as Danto called it in his seminal work, the *artworld*. Yet, the artworld would become, especially after the American philosopher George Dickie's interpretation of it, something very different from what Dante originally proposed. Dickie transformed Danto's atmosphere (the artworld for Danto would always and only be a theoretical atmosphere) into an outright institution, or rather, as we shall see further on, a 'quasi institution', a rather hazy establishment of vague outline, vested with the final decision-making power over the formulation of ontological and artistic judgements. Thus Danto provided Dickie with the theoretical germ for the development of the institutional theory of art, yet Danto's artworld in no way resembles Dickie's artworld. Rather, Danto's idea is that what we classify as art depends, among other things, on properties that are not perceptible via the senses, and hence they do not belong solely to the material aspect of the works, but instead depend on the theoretical context in which the art is developed. They are properties that the eye cannot descry, but which we effectively can grasp in other ways, through the intellect rather than the senses. Thus, if we have two indiscernible neckties, both a deep midnight blue in colour, one painted by a child at playtime, the other painted by Picasso, we can safely say that only the latter is a work of art, while the former, painted by the child, is not, despite the fact that the two neckties are physically identical and indiscernible from each other. In Danto's understanding of it, in such cases, which in many ways are similar to ready-mades, it is the relational and contextual properties, together with the subject's act of interpretation, which make the magic of art possible, enabling the two objects to be distinguished from an ontological perspective.[22]

It is without a doubt that Danto privileges semantic properties over aesthetic-perceptive ones. For him, what distinguishes a work of art from a mere thing which is otherwise indiscernible from it are properties that fall within the sphere of the meanings of the work, the intentionality of the artist, the cultural environment enabling the development of the artist's work, and so on. Considerations of the same kind also apply to works that are otherwise indiscernible. A celebrated example are the red squares that Danto cites in the opening pages of *The Transfiguration of the Commonplace*. It consists of an array of indiscernible canvases, all squares of red paint of the same identical shade, each distinguished by a different title. The array of red squares is a thought experiment of particular significance, also from a methodological point of view, as what Danto does with it is create a tabula rasa wiped clean of the various ways that art has been understood and classified over the centuries. Danto returns repeatedly to the array to argue the same point, that the characteristics that identify a work are its semantic properties—what the work is about, or its *aboutness*, together with its contextual properties. Hence, the metaphorical and stylistic structure of the work is important not for the formal qualities it implies, but for the ways in which it conveys semantic properties. Such a theory disenfranchises beauty in a major way, degrading the king of all aesthetic properties from a central role to an entirely marginal one in this context. In short, a work of art may be beautiful or ugly, or be neither

22 In relation to this specific point, Danto owes much to the work of Mandelbaum (1965).

beautiful nor ugly, but it cannot lack *aboutness*. Danto's argument is therefore a radical one, as it suggests shifting art from the sphere of aesthetics, in which Baumgarten (1961) placed it, to the general sphere of philosophy, in particular, semantics.

Those are, in a nutshell, the core questions addressed by Danto in a series of works that culminated in *The Transfiguration of the Commonplace*. It is noteworthy how the *Transfiguration* enlists studies developed by Danto over the previous decades in the fields of the philosophy of knowledge, the philosophy of history, and the philosophy of action. In the second-half of the 1980s, Danto added a series of other questions to his interest in more traditional ontological issues, which essentially addressed (a) the relationship of art with beauty; and (b) the question, of Hegelian inspiration and tied in some measure to Danto's youthful interest in the philosophy of history, concerning the end of art.

3.2.3 The Decline of Beauty and the End of Art

Danto developed early on very clear ideas about the question of beauty, which are consistent with his general theory and which tend to remove art from the sphere of aesthetics. To put it simply, since art primarily has to do with the sphere of meaning, and aesthetics predominantly concerns perception, aesthetics has no reason to investigate the domain of art. Thus, beauty is an ancillary property, as are aesthetic properties in general, which means there is no problem at all in conceiving of an art that is not beautiful, since beauty does not fall within the properties that an object must have to be a work of art (Ramljak et al. 2003). That artists have so often strived to achieve beauty can be explained by considering that, although beauty is not a necessary property from the point of view of definition, and hence it is not necessary from an ontological perspective, beauty is nevertheless an important property in all that concerns our experience of works, and hence our relationship with works of art. Given that works are about something, that they convey a certain *aboutness*, two types of beauty exist: internal beauty, which concerns the structure of the medium and which we appreciate every time we assert that a work is well made; and external beauty, which instead concerns the aesthetic properties of the work. Internal beauty is what brings a work of art to achieve goals of artefactual and stylistic perfection. We can safely say that Titian's *Crucifixion* is beautiful, despite the fact that the subject it represents incontrovertibly is not. It is beautiful in the sense that it shows outstanding technical mastery and represents its subject in such skilful ways as to enable the artist to achieve his purpose. The same can be said of a painting such as *Guernica*, by Pablo Picasso. It would be nonsensical to claim that it is a beautiful work, at least in the more common understanding of the term, which is given by external beauty. However, it does make sense to stress the internal beauty of the work, namely its ability to capture the intentions of the artist.

Having distinguished the two acceptations of beauty to which we refer when we talk about art, it is now necessary to consider the reasons that motivate the use of beauty in art. In other words, the question is why artists over the centuries have sought to create works that are pleasing in an aesthetic sense. The answer to that question relates not so much to the ontology of art, but rather, in all likelihood, to the sociology of art, which studies, among many other things, why art is of any interest to us. The reasons can be found in its capacity to convey emotions, and emotions are in many ways tied to beauty, as well as to the various properties that constitute its contrary. Thus it follows that works of art that are not at all beautiful certainly can, and do, exist, but also that beautiful works of art generally succeed in touching us in more direct and effective ways. Another question we might ask is whether art must necessarily touch us emotionally. The answer is, obviously, no, in the sense that there are absolute masterpieces that do not touch us at all—the twentieth century, in particular, and more than any other, produced a number of avant-garde movements that deliberately sought to strip art of beauty and emotion. On the other hand, however, especially in our capacity as audience, it pains us to forgo emotions in art. That is probably the case because although emotions in art are authentic, they are also highly convenient, in the sense that they do not entail the same sort of affective and cognitive commitment required by their indiscernible counterparts that populate our daily lives. Nevertheless, the fact is that contemporary art has sought to disassociate itself from beauty, much like someone might seek to disassociate from a partner of great celebrity. And the reason for that disassociation is probably to be found in the need felt by artists to assert their substantial independence from the wishes and needs of art patrons.

Danto's deconstruction of beauty and of the legitimacy of its role in art is closely tied to the question of the death of art, anticipated in his own way by Hegel. In Danto's conception of it, it is not really the lack of beauty, or the inability to produce beauty, which has lead to the decline of Western art—a decline that started in the twentieth century and for which the twenty-first century has yet to find an convincing explanation. If beauty, as Danto argues, is not a defining property of art, then ultimately it makes no difference whether it is there or not. What has brought about the end of art is that its historical development has come to an end. It has reached its culmination, beyond which there can be no history. Thus the end of art is not really the end of art itself, but of the Vasarian narrative of the history of the arts. Danto's theory is quite simple in many ways and partially consistent with his philosophy of history, as developed in the *Analytical Philosophy of History*. It argues that the narrative developed by Vasari, namely, the historical-interpretive account that has come to constitute the paradigm of the history of Western art, which understands art as a discipline that grows and progresses, is destined to reach stagnation and exhaustion. Having reached the culmination of its possibilities for technical and expressive development, at the turn of the twentieth century the diversification and enrichment of artistic practices in part transformed, and in part expanded the identity of art as a discipline. What we consider art today is often quite eccentric in character compared to the Vasarian theory. The process is an irreversible one, which Danto describes by observing it from the stretch of history in which it took place, and hence from its conclusion, which enables, from a logical point of view, Danto's theoretical inquiry and the consequent formulation of a philosophy of the history of art.

3.3 *Institutional Theory: Art as Stipulation*

The philosophers William Kennick (1958) and Morris Weitz (1956) have argued that there are cases in which a noun is simply a rather broad label, useful for encompassing a number of concepts that are ultimately quite diverse. In itself, the theory is not new. Generally speaking, it is the same approach taken, for example, by Nietzsche, when he asks us to consider language as the outcome of a series of semantic stratifications. Thus, the good does not exist in and of itself; rather there are various ways in which ethical and moral theories characterize and conceptualize behaviour, deriving the concepts of good and evil. Similarly, there is no such thing as art in and of itself (from which it follows that no definition of it is possible); rather there are different forms of artistic production, or different ways of making art. Then there is the second theoretical point raised by Weitz, which is that since artistic production is incessant and always new, it would appear logically impossible to define the concept.[23]

Such theories introduce the idea for which art is substantially the result of a process of stipulation, effected on a conventional and cultural basis. It is that assumption that forms the starting point for George Dickie, the father of the institutional theory (IT) of art. Dickie focused his inquiry of on two aspects. On the one hand, he sought to identify the agents that belong to the artworld and perform some sort of institutional task; on the other, he sought to clarify the structure of the stipulation process. Dickie is another thinker, much like

23 Interesting criticisms have been raised against Weitz's argument by Tatarkiewicz (1980, 33–34) and, more recently, by Goehr (2007).

Danto, who takes an antagonistic stance in the development of his philosophy against what was a strong theory very much in vogue. If for Danto the adversary was the mimetic theory of art, for Dickie it was the theory of aesthetic attitude, which is the theory that identifies the key for distinguishing what is art from what is not in the attitude of the observer.

Two pillars underpin Dickie's institutional theory of art. The first concerns the property that defines art as such, what in technical terms can be identified as the necessary property (or properties) of art. That property is artefactuality, or the fact that works of art are necessarily artefacts, in one sense or another. The second pillar is instead an offshoot of Danto's essentialist theory, and builds specifically on the idea that the artworld performs a decisive function in establishing what is art (Dickie 1969). Dickie's underlying thesis, which, as we said, draws from and develops in original ways Danto's previous insight, is that the social context, which largely corresponds to the artworld, is decisive in shaping what we consider to be art. It is curious that Dickie's understanding of the artworld gives specification to a theoretical atmosphere which, in "The Artworld", Danto deliberately treated as vague. Despite Dickie's intentions, the difference between their two understandings is clear and consistent. The point that Dickie most certainly misunderstood, and which Danto intentionally left indeterminate, is that the artworld is defined as a theoretical atmosphere. In Dickie's conception of it, the artworld coincides with a set of practices, procedures, and agents that constitute the artworld itself. Essentially, therefore, Dickie's artworld is a solid entity, embodied in the institutional, or quasi-institutional, practices of its agents, whereas Danto's artworld is rarefied and diffuse, corresponding to something that is entirely theoretical. The theoretical atmosphere to which Danto refers, and as Danto explained it in his later writings, essentially concerns the relational and historical properties that fully belong to the ontology of the work of art, in the same way that semantic properties and formal properties do. Dickie instead interprets that theoretical atmosphere as though it were something eminently social, and hence institutional. Thus he claims, from a descriptivist perspective, that a work of art is an artefact upon which a society, or a sub-group of a society, has conferred the status of candidate for appreciation (1969, 254).

In Dickie's view, therefore, works of art are artefacts whose identity—their being candidates for appreciation—is established by agents with a decision-making role in the artworld. Accordingly, Dickie identifies two immediate objectives for his theory to address: the first is to provide a plausible explanation of the introduction of ready-mades in the class of art works (1978, 32–44); the second is to discuss the weaknesses of one of the most accredited theories of art at the time Dickie was writing, which was the theory of aesthetic attitude.[24] By applying the theory of aesthetic attitude to the ontological problems raised by ready-mades, Dickie sought to conclude that the reason why we can consider a ready-made a work of art is connected to a particular attitude (the aesthetic attitude) that enables us to view the object in a different way to how we typically would in everyday behaviour. Hence, the theory is valid for all the arts, and not just the visual arts. Indeed, it is precisely the aesthetic attitude that stops us from running away when we watch a horror film, or from rushing to prevent Medea from killing her children. The aesthetic attitude, therefore, is purported to be that typically human attitude that enables us to create worlds of imagination and to make specific judgements for their interpretation. Thus it is essentially a mental disposition.

With Bell's framework in mind and the developments witnessed in the art works of his time, Dickie produces two different definitions of art, both of which revolve around the artefactual nature of works and the artworld understood as an institutional framework (Dickie and Rump 1978, 41).[25] The first definition reads as follows:

> A work of art in the descriptive sense is (1) an artifact (2) upon which some society or sub-group of a society has conferred the status of candidate for appreciation".
>
> DICKIE 1969, 254

In the second definition, Dickie introduces certain variants:

> A work of art in a classificatory sense is (1) an artifact (2) upon which some person or persons acting on behalf of a certain social institution (the art world) has conferred the status of candidate for appreciation.
>
> DICKIE AND SCLAFANI 1977, 197

In contrast to the first formulation, the 1977 definition makes explicit reference to the artworld as a social institution. That second and more complete formulation of the theory is therefore underpinned by three pillars, namely: a) the fact that works of art are artefacts, which means, given current definitions of artefactuality, that they are objects that have been modified or produced

24 In the Anglo-American tradition in which Dickie worked, the reference is quite patently to the work of Bell (1924).

25 For a discussion and development of Dickie's institutional theory see Cohen (1973).

intentionally to serve a certain purpose;[26] b) the fact that as artefacts they are candidates for appreciation, which means they are able to elicit a certain interest in and relationship with the work that prescind from the aesthetic dimension; and finally, c) the idea that institutions play a decisive role in determining what is art and what is not by conferring the possibility of appreciation; that is, they have the authority and power, exercised through various means of an institutional and cultural nature (specialist journals, art galleries, museums, and specialist studies, etc.), to confer the possibility of appreciation on an object. This last point is particularly insidious for two fundamental reasons. First of all, because the various institutional agents that Dickie has in mind carry out practices that are not very normative in nature and, all things considered, rather fast and loose. Secondly, because it would appear necessary to presuppose a certain circularity between the artworld, which needs works of art to exist, and works of art, which in turn need the artworld to be acknowledged as such. It may well be, as Dickie himself argues, that circularity lies in things; however, it is fair to say, at first instance at least, that philosophy cannot accept a circular explanation.

It is clear that, in his theoretical framework, Dickie leaves ample room for action and ample power to the artworld, consisting of the practices and agents that act in all the various domains that concern the arts. In a certain sense, the domains of philosophy that traditionally have investigated art have little to say or contribute to the theoretical questions posited by Dickie. At the same time, however, it is important to note how Dickie draws on, despite remaining rather vague as to the details of his theory, fields of philosophy that generally have little to do with art, and which instead address the question of institutions and how they work. One specific example is social ontology. Within the philosophical framework constructed in his 1974 work and then developed and in part amended in the later work *The Art Circle: A Theory of Art* (1984), Dickie makes reference to the socio-institutional context to account for the changes introduced in art history by avant-garde art and the Dada movement. To illustrate those changes, which primarily affected the sphere of art production, and hence the ontology of the arts, Dickie stresses the role and functioning of an institutional, or quasi-institutional, context, which he identifies as the artworld. In that sense, the question 'What is art?' is effectively reformulated on a different level to become, broadly, 'How are the institutional mechanisms that enable the creation of art structured?' Neither aesthetics nor the philosophy

26 Hilpinen, Risto, "Artifact", *The Stanford Encyclopedia of Philosophy* (Winter 2011 Edition), Edward N. Zalta (ed.), URL = <https://plato.stanford.edu/archives/win2011/entries/artifact/>.

of art were obviously equipped to answer that question, and the institutional theory exposes all their limitations. The central theoretical question is not, therefore, the inquiry into the nature of art and its products, but rather the inquiry into the mechanisms for conferring that something which we traditionally call 'artisticness' and which Dickie identifies with appreciation. We are talking, for all intents and purposes, about a mechanism for conferring status, something very similar to the process identified by John Searle as the practice of constituting social reality.

Precisely that last point, however, is particularly problematic. It is no coincidence that Dickie again draws on the concept of artworld, treating it as a concept that is intrinsically vague, even after having conceived it as an institution. The artworld is ascribed a certain capacity to articulate critical judgement and, consequently, a certain agency in relation to the sphere of art. More precisely, the artworld purportedly determines, according to procedures that depend, from time to time, on the agents involved, which objects presented for its judgement can be candidates for appreciation. Thus appreciation, which is not necessarily aesthetic in nature, is dependent on an 'institutional subject', but in a way that is fundamentally different from the dependency that exists between a subject and aesthetic experience. In this framework, understanding the dynamics that govern the assignment of function becomes fundamental. In other words, while aesthetic experience is made possible by the relationship between subject and object (the rising of the sun is a scene that raises the possibility of a precise emotional and cognitive state in a person), artistic experience would appear to made possible by knowledge that is preliminary to the experience itself, knowledge that depends not only on the artistic object, at least as concerns its coming into being. In Dickie's institutional theory, the role of the artworld is precisely that of establishing preliminarily, through the assignment of function, which artefacts can give rise to artistic experience. All of which assumes as an underlying condition that the aesthetic and artistic domains should remain distinct. In fact, if we assume that the aesthetic sphere is determined predominantly by perceptive dynamics and is not limited to the artistic domain, and that, vice versa, the artistic sphere privileges cognitive dynamics referring strictly to the domain of art, then Dickie's distinction becomes clearer, in one sense, and perhaps even more sustainable, in another. It is obviously a matter of understanding the aspects involved in the assignment of function and the power dynamics that are part and parcel of assignment processes for functions of an institutional nature. More generally, it should be stressed how the mechanism for assigning function, a process of an intrinsically formal nature, is weakly dependent on the object, but strongly dependent on the people who determine it. In other words, we are dealing with a process that is only weakly tied to the intrinsic and relational properties of the artefact. Thus it is of extreme interest to understand who can activate it and who can effect the actions needed to realize it and finalize it, and to understand its dynamics as a whole.

The general rule for processes of assigning function was formulated by John Searle in *The Construction of Social Reality* (1995, 40ff). There he states it as "X counts as Y in C", which means that a certain thing counts as a different thing—i.e., it assumes a different function to its original function—in a given context. The rule appears to explain very clearly what happens in the case of ready-made works of art: 'a urinal counts as a work of art in the contemporary Western artworld'. We know what a urinal is—an artefact built to fulfil a specific function—but we do not possess a similarly precise definition of a work of art or, to stress again, the artworld. In a sense, that renders the assignment of function rather simple, as we do not have any particularly strict conditions to satisfy. Having said that, however, it is evident that once we have clarified the rule determining how social reality functions and, therefore, the artworld, understood as a precise aspect (or sub-aspect) of the social world, the next step is to inquire into those dynamics. At which point, it will become crucial to address questions of the sort, who can act in such a way as to impose a function? Or rather, who is it that has that special kind of power? It is clear how referring to the artworld becomes strategic—it is the artworld, in all its various and numerous components, that makes the assignment of function possible. That is, it is those who belong to that micro-social world who hold the power necessary to determine the change of function. To put it in more concrete terms, it is the museum director, the art critic, the art historian, the authoritative art journal, or a combination of all those agents and other people we can imagine or who can in some way step in at a certain point, who have the capacity to change the function and status of, or add a function and status to, a certain artefact. Furthermore, since the artworld, granted that it can be considered a meta-institution or a set of institutions of various kinds, is highly fluid in character, it is obvious that the dynamics that govern it will necessarily be fluid as well, and, in part, very difficult to codify. For instance, it remains undetermined which of the artworld agents will have the final say in deciding whether a problematic artefact can be included in the class of works of art. Is it the artist? The critic? The public? Or is it, rather, the outcome of the cooperation of various agents? Marcel Duchamp's *Fountain*, the ready-made he 'created' in 1917 is a significant case in point. As we know, the French artist selected the object by purchasing it from a Manhattan store to submit it to a young artists competition run by the Society of Independent Artists. The judges, consisting of a panel of experts, namely the institutional agents imagined by Dickie, refused the work on the precise and simple grounds that *Fountain* could not be submitted to the competition because it was not a work of art. It was then that the artist took up pen and paper to explain his motivations.

What is significant here for our purposes is the conflict in decision-making and normative powers that led to the exclusion of *Fountain* from the competition. Who has the authority, and hence the power, necessary to determine that 'X counts as Y in context C'? At first glance it would appear not to have been the artist, who saw his *Fountain* excluded from the class of works. Note that what we have is not a case of *Fountain* being judged a bad work of art, or a work of art of poor quality. Rather, it is a case of expert judges asserting, logically to say the least, their normative and decision-making power while not being at all in agreement with the maker of the work. In that case, the artworld—at the start of the affair, at least—had a greater say than the artist. In the end, what emerges is how the decision concerning what is art and what is not effectively depended on an act of stipulation, which in turn depended on agents, who can vary depending on the institutional relationships and power relationships expressed by the artworld. Thus what we have is the idea that the domain of art is, by its nature, fluid—a consideration that goes hand in hand with another classic consideration in this theoretical context, which is the idea that since artistic production is incessant and constantly exhibits new characteristics, then it is in fact impossible to standardize it through the identification of necessary and sufficient properties. Hence it would appear we find ourselves in the case in which institutional, or quasi-institutional, entities are able to make choices that cannot be disputed, since those choices are made on the basis of rather loose criteria.

As much as we can concede to the idea of stipulation, two things remain to be clarified. First, whether everything, or almost everything, is really left to stipulation, as would seem to emerge from Dickie's theory, or if there are properties that restrict it, a bit like how interpretation is restricted by a text and required to respect its basic content. Thus it is not just a matter of understanding whether stipulation plays some role, given that it seems fairly clear that it does and a certain margin for stipulation evidently exists, but rather of understanding what, if any, are the limits of stipulation practices and whether those limits are strict. Secondly, there is the matter of understanding which agents can play some sort of role in the great game of the artworld.

3.4 *The Historical-Contextual Approach*

The institutional theory is based on the insight that the institutional context—whatever that means—plays a decisive role in distinguishing what is art from what is not. Yet, as Dickie developed it, the idea remains rather sketchy. Those are the issues that set the stage for the work of Jerrold Levinson, which seeks to correct the institutional theory by underscoring the role played by time in the development of the practices of agents who, in fulfilling more or less institutionalised functions, engage with art. Time dependence in Levinson assumes the characteristics of historical development—the idea that the artworld has sharpened its identity through a narrative of the changes that have shaped artistic practices, which show, on the one hand, a certain continuity from a historical perspective, and development, on the other, in techniques. Thus, precisely because the concept of artworld is substantially so difficult to define, or even just outline in a positive way, at least from the perspective proposed by Dickie, Levinson proposes replacing it with a notion that is intrinsically better defined and more traditional, namely, an art history that is non-institutional and even unself-conscious (Levinson 1989, 22ff).

As Levinson sees it, in art there is never a complete break with the paradigm. Even in instances of what appear to be radical transformations, there is always a connection with the traditional narrative. Thus the thread that links past, present, and future is never completely severed; at most it is reconfigured in novel ways. Such reconfiguration is what makes artistic creation possible, without requiring the introduction of any act of conferring status. Levinson's position takes up Danto's suggestion of highlighting the importance of the historical-theoretical component, for if we were to define the atmosphere to which Danto refers in his 1964 work in positive terms, there are two fundamental components we could identify: theories of art and the historical-cultural context in which art grows and develops. Within that framework, Levinson proposes a definition grounded in three fundamental conditions: 1) artistic intentionality (expressed by an individual or by a group); (2) an institutional setting, corresponding to a concept of the artworld that is time dependent, as we said earlier; and, finally, (3) reference to an informed context as to artistic practices and the history of art. Levinson provides three formulations of his theory, which are essentially three successive formulations aimed at bringing about a definition through the emergence, and hence inclusion, of successive qualifications. The first formulation states:

> (I) X is an artwork at t = df X is an object which a person or persons having the appropriate proprietary right over X, non-passingly intends for regarded-as-a-work-of-art, i.e. regard in any way (or ways) in which prior art works are or were correctly (or standardly) regarded.
>
> LEVINSON, 230

The first definition clearly centres on intentionality and the question of proprietary rights over the object. Intentionality must therefore be stable, while proprietary rights are indispensable for an object to be disposed of appropriately and completely. The first definition is formulated in such a way as to make it impossible for an artistic judgement made at t2 to effect any radical change on the canon by demanding the exclusion from the canon itself of an object that was already regarded as a work of art. Suppose, for example, that at some time in the future tastes were to change in such a way as to demand that the works of the Impressionist painters no longer be regarded as works of art, but as simple colour tests. For Levinson, such a declassification of a work to mere object (canvas for colour testing) cannot be permitted.

The second and third formulations of the definition underscore, respectively, the dependency of works on the canon, and hence their connection with the history that produces them, and how the class of objects to which works of art belong should be intended. Thus the second definition states:

> (I1) X is an artwork at t = df X is an object of which it is true at t that some person or persons having the appropriate proprietary right over X, non-passingly intends (or intended) X for regarded-as-a-work-of-art, i.e. regard in any way (or ways) in which art works existing prior to t are or were correctly (or standardly) regarded;
>
> LEVINSON 1979, 238

and the third definition:

> (I1') X is an artwork at t = df X is an object of which it is true at t that some person or persons having the appropriate proprietary right over X, non-passingly intends (or intended) X for regarded-as-a-work-of-art, *i.e.* regard in any way (or ways) in which objects in the extension of 'art works' existing prior to t are or were correctly (or standardly) regarded.
>
> LEVINSON, 240

Levinson clearly intends to bypass the critical elements typical of institutional positions (essentially, the concept of artworld in Dickie's formulation of it and the idea of institutional action) by undergirding the institutional theory with a different set of pillars, namely: intentionality, which takes on a much broader range of meanings and uses than in Dickie's argument; the candidates entitled to make artistic judgements of objects; and, finally, the artistic canon, which constitutes the condition for the possibility and identity of art. In Levinson's conception of it, the artistic canon can be progressively expanded but never broken with in a definitive way—which is like saying that works of art are connected to each other by an underlying thread which can clearly be traced in a work of art or, where it is reduced to its essentials, in the intention of the artist, who engages with the canon even if only to deconstruct it.

The central theoretical point, therefore, is the change in the identity of an object—for in Levinson, as in the other theories we have examined thus far, the work of art retains its object-hood—which shows the same properties from a phenomenal perspective but which, with time, is interpreted and classified in different ways from an ontological perspective. Hence, the problem is one of identity over time. How can we explain the change in status, and hence in classification, of one and the same object that, for instance, is classified at time t as a historical artefact and at time t1 as a work of art? A classic example are icons, conceived as objects for the purposes of worship at one time, and then interpreted as works of art at a later stage of their history. Another is the case of ready-mades, objects built as everyday objects and, therefore, to fulfil certain specific functions, which in some cases become works of art.

From the point of view of metaphysics, there are more or less two theoretical strategies available in response to that problem. One is to locate in the change of status the cause of the change in ontological classification; the other focuses on the need to reflect on the relational properties and the elements that in some way constitute the frame of the artworld, and which also carry a major weight in the determination of the classification. To explain the change in the ontology of a work of art, therefore, it is necessary to understand in what ways, and in relation to which properties, time dependence affects the object. Levinson's idea is that it happens through a remodulation, over time, of the three factors we mentioned earlier—of the intentionality underlying the construction of an object, which can be construed in different ways over time. Levinson's specific approach affords particularly ample room for such interpretation, suggesting the possibility of a sort of hermeneutic revision of the artist's intention. He holds that artistic intentionality can, so to speak, be attributed ex-post, through an interpretive act (Levinson 1979, 238ff). It is an intentionality, we might say, that can assume an artistic character even without the artist knowing it, and can be attributed by the interpreter, or those who have the power to make such an attribution. Thus, the change in classification appears to be motivated by an act of interpretation and justified by the vaster cultural context in which art is embedded. In short, *Fountain* was made possible by the American art context in the latter part of the twentieth century, which therefore makes it a necessary condition for the work, but also by the precedent history of art, which enabled avant-garde movements in art to emerge. That is true for the more controversial cases, just as it is for works lying within the mainstream of the art historical tradition.

The emphasis placed on time dependence enables Levinson to reduce the internal fractures in the tradition of art and, as a consequence, the number of critical ontological issues. It is clear that the prevalent strategy of his argument is to strengthen the continuity of the artistic canon and bring all works of art within its fold—even the most eccentric with respect to the canon. And in practice, the canon must have the openness and elasticity necessary to encompass and, at the same time, account for all creative eccentricities. The argument is that even in the case of art works that least appear reducible to the tradition, the artist referred to that tradition, even if only in conceiving of himself as an artist. The idea here, essentially, is that all deconstruction processes are in some way parasitic on construction (hence, on the canon) to be able to effect deconstruction, which means that deconstruction is obviously destined to remain within the canon it deconstructs. As such, it makes no sense, from this perspective at least, to conceive of an end of art.

4 What a Work of Art Is

4.1 *As Concerns Necessary Conditions*

In many ways, our discussion so far has looked at only part of the picture. Of the numerous theories that have been developed over the centuries to explain what art is and the purpose it serves and to address the metaphysical, ontological, and value issues it entails, here we have selected only a sample of particular theoretical import. At first glance, it is perhaps striking that art—something so immediately grasped in many ways by common sense—should demand such explanatory efforts from philosophy. Yet that is because what would seem to be the 'simplest answer' to the ontological question of art just does not appear to work. The simplest answer, one that is even simpler than that offered by imitation theory, is captured by Dominic McIver Lopes in these terms: "item x is a work of art if and only if x is a work in activity *P* and *P* is one of the arts" (Lopes 2008, 109), where *P* obviously stands for any one of the arts, including painting, sculpture, music, literature, dance, theatre, and film. Lopes argues that the simplest answer—i.e., that art is what belongs to the class of activities considered to be artistic, which for convenience are classified under different genres—is also the right one. What that ultimately means is that there is no need to explore matters of definition because it is necessary and sufficient to look at the activities which we associate in any way with artistic production.[27] The rest, as Kristeller suggests (1951), is the fruit of a stipulation made much later and motivated by the practical needs of giving order to a field, to what we today call the world of art, which was becoming increasingly composite. Such

27 It would be proper here to mention that the opposite view is also held and well developed in the literature; see, for example, Annelies Monseré (2016).

ideas, which are well known and widely exemplified in the literature, emphasize how the concept of art is irrelevant for the production of art,[28] while also emphasizing the irrelevance of the concept of intentionality. Lopes, therefore, holds that the simple answer is the right one, and what is needed instead is to understand how to address in the most appropriate way the questions that lead to the formulation of the simplest answer.

In view of all that, and considering, additionally, the contributions made by the various theories that have sought to explain art from various perspectives, we can see that any inquiry into the identity of art must consider a variety of elements. Recent theories have accepted that fact and, for the most part, have focused more stably on a multidimensional perspective aimed at identifying the set of conditions necessary to establish the concept of art. I suggest that an initial list of necessary conditions, which we shall call *standard conditions*, for what is art, should include:

1. *an object* (i.e., a work of art);
2. *subjects* (in the dual sense of the artist and the audience);
3. *a space for possibility* (or *aboutness*, what the work is *about*);
4. *normativity* (meaning the vast set of rules, conventions, and usages that shape artistic practice and, in the better cases, enable the formation of a style);
5. *institutional frameworks* (meaning the dynamics of the context, which may be more or less institutional and institutionalized, and generally encompass a diverse array of types and forms of patronage, for whom a work of art has meaning and value);
6. *a story* (or a narrative that revolves around art);
7. *a market* (meaning the supply and demand for works of art, the dynamics of which in the contemporary world have assumed many of the typical characteristics of financial markets, coexisting with and at times replacing more traditional forms of trade).[29]

These seven conditions, all of which are necessary conditions, as we said, are fairly stable, in the sense that they can be found in all ages, whatever the concept of art adopted. Here we shall focus on the first four conditions, which

28 See, for example, Shiner (2001), Davies (2005), and Lopes (2007).

29 For an initial discussion of the analogies that exist between the worlds of contemporary art and finance, through an examination of Tulip Mania, history's first ever speculative bubble, see Andina (2013, 51ff.).

pertain to a work or the space of the work (they are, substantially, internal conditions to the work), whereas the last three conditions, which are, so to speak, external to the work, shall not be addressed. Although the elements in question are all fairly standard, their significance has differed in different eras of artistic production, which is probably the reason why the concept of art has known so many variations, of greater or lesser degree, over the centuries, which in turn caused artistic practices to change. It also explains why it has taken so long for most of the necessary conditions shaping the concept of art to emerge. The idea, therefore, is that, with regard to our list of necessary conditions, rather than introducing radical novelties, or radically new conditions, contemporary art, understood as the many currents of art that have taken shape since the beginning of the twentieth century, has either (a) embodied the standard conditions differently, or (b) interpreted the standard conditions in radically different terms, or (c) ascribed a different and non-traditional weight to each of the standard conditions. A more in-depth analysis of the first four standard conditions can help us explain the point better.

4.2 *The Standard Conditions and Their Variations*

We said that the standard conditions have been interpreted and embodied in different ways, which means that they have opened up varying margins of freedom and action for the various agents of the artworld. Let us look at the point more analytically.

(1) *An object.* A work of art has always been, first and foremost, an artefact. That means it is an object built and modified on the basis of an explicit intention by the artist, to serve some imaginative, creative, communicative, or simply expressive purpose. It is no coincidence that if we go back to the beginnings of history, the roots of art are found in technique, or in the technical component required to achieve certain practices (the art of medicine, for instance, or of the scientist, or engineering practices) or certain artefacts (technical skill, and hence, in a figurative sense, art is needed to build a bed, whether it is crafted by a skilled joiner or, as is more frequently the case, mass produced, just as it is required to create a painting of a bed or a bed produced by decisively less traditional artistic practices, such as those of Rauschenberg and Oldenburg). The creation of artefacts was strongly tied to idea of technique being applied to 'something', and that something can be interpreted as an object existing in space and time. It can be a sound object, a literary object, or even a physical object, such as a picture, but that does not change the point—their construction requires specific technical skills, which have developed and evolved and require a field of application. That field is the art object, in all its different and possible embodiments.

It follows that a work of art is something found in the world and which maintains its identity from an ontological perspective and a sort of independence from the artist—as is exemplified by *Document*, the work by Robert Morris which we discussed earlier, where the artist, for reasons of a completely contingent nature, was driven by a desire to disown his work. He quite obviously failed in his intent, but the case raises a series of compelling questions about whether an artist, or who acts, say, on his behalf, can claim the right to restore a work of art to the state of non-being, also as concerns its authorship. Suppose we considered it sustainable to hold that a work of art should be protected from what the artist does or decides to do—Francis Bacon, for instance, would regularly attempt to destroy his portraits after painting them. Then we would also have to be prepared to separate a work from the concept of authorship. That all poses questions of undeniable interest about whether a work of art can be altered without substantially changing its identity. To what extent can we interfere with an original, for conservation purposes, for instance, or to restore the body of the work? For our standard conditions, is the artefact only the original work, or can alterations be tolerated—and if so, what sort? Important points are raised in this regard by restoration practices in use in Asian countries, as well as the growing body of thought regarding the restoration of contemporary art.[30] In both cases, albeit for different reasons, restoration would appear to be impossible. For the Asian world, the body of a work, for theoretical and cultural reasons, cannot appear to endure variations, unless minimal.[31] In Asian countries, it seems, the paradox of the ship of Theseus is resolved in restoration circles by opting for the conservative answer.

---

30 For an interesting analysis, see Irvin (2005), who argues that artists impose certain parameters upon art works and those parameters help us understand to which category a particular art work belongs.

31 The Ship of Theseus was put forward as a philosophical paradox in the seventeenth century by Thomas Hobbes (1650), who took it from the story told by Plutarch in the *Life of Theseus*. Plutarch recounts that the ship on which Theseus returned from his mission to Crete was preserved as a whole and used for religious rites for many years, with each piece replaced over time as it decayed. Hobbes asks us to imagine the case in which the repairs are such as to enable the ship to survive long enough that at a certain point it consists exclusively of new parts and none of the original planks that constituted it are a part of it any more. Which leads him to ask, 'Is the ship consisting entirely of new timber still the same Ship of Theseus?' Hobbes then complicated the thought experiment further by imagining that there is someone tasked with gathering all the replaced parts so that, once the last piece of Theseus' ship is replaced, a new ship consisting entirely of the original parts could be built. At that point, the question becomes, 'Is the new ship built from the replaced parts still the same Ship of Theseus?'

In the case of contemporary art, the idea itself of restoration is, in some cases, extremely problematic, as some artists believe it necessary that a work should be left to decay until its complete destruction. As Michelangelo Pistoletto effectively explained in an interview given in 1986:

> As regards my own works, they represent the change in things, that is, a shift. It is like a candle that burns but substitutes itself. There is a change that lies very close to nature—it is the possibility of continuous substitution that nature itself has. In these works, there is precisely a desire for renewal and change. It is like the image in the mirror, which has a life of its own and always renews itself. In my work, there is an evident participation in the life process and I would say that Arte Povera itself shows that rationale.
>
> ANGELUCCI 1994, 197

While idea that art is tied to artefactuality was virtually unquestionable until the turn of the twentieth century, developments in the latter half of the 1900s raised a number of interesting ontological issues. One issue to emerge was that the notion itself of the object, understood as artefact, as a vehicle for conveying aboutness is in many ways too restrictive. That led to the standard conditions being reviewed in part in relation to ontology, with the introduction, alongside the notion of an object, of the concept of action and, in general, event. The work of art thus assumed the character of event and performance, stressing the central importance of its extension in time. With a performance, for example, the work develops over time and is consumed by time, all of which happens systematically by the design of the artist. In that case, the work exhibits the typical character of an event, for which the ontology of art has to be equipped with the concepts of action and, as the case may be, of artistic action.

The 2015 Venice Biennale was won by the Afro-American conceptual artist and philosopher Adrian Piper. Piper is an analytic philosopher, who has taught at the prestigious universities of Georgetown, Harvard, and Stanford. She is a Kant scholar with a particular interest in metaethics, and she has worked on the problem of the constitution of personal identity and how it is conditioned by interaction with others. *The Probable Trust Registry* is the work she presented at the Biennale. The work is a performance, which uses a theatrical style of narration to show the dynamics of interpersonal bonds and social contracts, highlighting their paradoxical aspects. In a setting reminiscent of the foyer of a large corporation building, visitors are called on to sign statements (such as, "I hereby declare that I will always do what I say I am going to do") in which they promise to take moral responsibility towards themselves and others. The statements are then photocopied and archived at the Adrian Piper Research Archive (APRA) Foundation in Berlin, constituting the actual work of art, which therefore consists of the voluntary acts of the signatories of the promises and of the written, documentary legacy that constitutes the tangible evidence and memory of those promises. *The Probable Trust Registry* could have been set up in various different ways and the technical skills necessary to perform the work are not traditional, yet the moral is exactly the same as in *Document*: the two works exhibit in an immediate way the structure and paradoxes of the social world, its normativity, and its practices. But while *Document* makes use of a traditional medium, namely a physical object, organised in a somewhat unconventional way, *The Probable Trust Registry* is instead organised around various different components—actions, documentary evidence collected in an archive, performance artists and simple individuals who act with greater or lesser awareness within the setting created by the artist and following her instructions, a space identified by a functional marker (the Biennale), and so on.

In such varied and multiform contexts, at the ontological level, action has come to have a significance equivalent to that enjoyed by artefactuality over the centuries. The performative dimension has enriched the ontology of art in a major way, but there are other forms of art which have risen in importance and are in a way even less 'concrete', in the sense that they prescind from the physical component traditionally associated with art. That is the case, for instance, with participatory art and relational practices. Relational practices are numerous and, to follow the description offered by Claire Bishop (2005), include socially engaged art, community-based art, experimental communities, dialogic art, littoral art, research-based art, and collaborative art. Such practices take no interest in the production of particular kinds of objects, but instead see art as an activity designed to give rise to collaborative practices. They are, ultimately, an alternative avant-garde that has spread and become consolidated since the 1990s, more or less, outside traditional artworld circles. Their primary aim is to emphasize the establishment of renewed forms of sociality through collaborative and concerted practices.[32] Activating collective practices, tied to the creation of community, therefore means diminishing the importance of key figures in the imagination of art, such as the maker-creator, as well as the importance of the 'work of art' as an object that endures in time and carries absolute value, and placing the focus instead on depersonalized and aggregating practices in art.[33] Thus we see a shift from the idea of

32 For a discussion of the questions raised by relational art see Bishop (2012), Bourriaud (2002), and Kester (2004).

33 See, above all, Bishop (2012).

individual authorship to the idea of distributed and participatory authorship, from which the work—no longer just an object but commonly a practice, action, or performance—emerges exhibiting unexpected and synergic aspects.

Such a profound reinterpretation touches the ontology of works as much as it does the role and function of some of the more significant agents of the artworld—first and foremost the artist, especially the romantic understanding of the concept of artist, which has long underpinned the strength of the concept. And, obviously, it invests the king of all aesthetic properties, beauty. The idea of beauty was put to the test in various ways over the course of the twentieth century. One challenge came from idea of showing that it is possible to produce art without beauty (typically attempted and theorized by Duchamp); another was to show that it is possible to produce art associated with an acceptation of beauty that has little to do with the aspectual properties of the object. So, just as ontology was revisited and the medium, understood as material object, gave way to performative acts, beauty has been shown to be less about perceptible properties and more of an abstract idea, generally corresponding not only to what is perceived visually but to what is grasped by the spirit to be particularly essential, harmonious, and, in a sense, perfect.[34] What has been witnessed, it should be stressed, is the emergence of a series of practices that have broadened the range of possibilities for art to explore, and not the introduction of a new normativity aimed at invalidating that of the tradition. That means that *if*, for example, it is possible to make art without recourse to beauty and by drawing on a different, and in a sense more complex notion of authorship, *then* it is important for all theorists of art to take these possibilities into account and incorporate them into their theories, so that they contemplate the aspects of the artworld that have emerged with the neo-avant-gardes.

The standard condition regarding object-hood thus proves to be ineffective and insufficient. Any revision of it, however, appears to suggest the need to review the concept itself of medium[35]—the idea of the work as an artefact that endures in time—to encompass other, alternative models that include action, performativeness, and coordinated collective action. In such cases, aboutness is embodied in a practice rather than an object, it belongs to a plurality of individuals and not to a single artist, and it conveys a precise emotional dimension that is central to and generative of meaning and emotion. A profound revision

34 On the question of beauty see, exemplarily, Danto (2003).

35 On the question of how the medium was pushed into the background by transformations in art as of the 1960s see Krauss (1999; 2000).

of the ontology of art, as recommended by the art of the neo-avant-garde,[36] has implications that affect not only the concept of art, but also its function. In short, it appears the question 'What is art?' cannot be separated from the question 'Why does it interest us?', which asks why art is so important not only for us, but for all cultures in all ages. While the question of what art is concerns ontology, the question of its function expressly concerns epistemology. Art interests us because it is through art that we can access a special sort of knowledge, connected with exemplariness.[37] Through art we apprehend objects that are exemplary, often in exemplary ways, which permit us to apply the knowledge acquired in useful ways in the specific functional domain of art and in ordinary reality. Thus, the function of art is to lead us to develop a kind of knowledge connected with *exempla*.

(2) *The subject* (*and its density*). In reality, it would, perhaps, be more appropriate to speak of subjects, as generally, in the case of art, we refer to at least two types of subjects. First there is the artist(s), who intentionally create(s) the work and whose intentionality is directed at artistic action; and then there is the audience, who receive the work and enjoy it. Artists and the audience are subjects in an eminent sense, but alongside them are a series of agents, people who play some sort of role in relation to the practices involved in the production of art. In some cases, they are agents who merely play a circumscribed role of little relevance to the life of a work of art; in others, they are agents who, besides the institutional roles they cover, perform functions that are fundamental for a work of art to be recognized, valued, and employed in the cultural sphere. Generally, however, the two types of subjects of real interest for art are those who make or participate in the making of art (we shall see how, especially with certain forms of art, this distinction plays a key role) and those who actively enjoy art. Therefore the subjects are the active agents who create or contribute to the creation of the work and its coming into being, and the somewhat passive agents who enjoy art.

If we were to delve into a sociology of art, what would not fail to strike us is how the idea of the artist and the idea of the audience have been understood in very different ways over the course of the centuries. Considering the matter from the side of the art maker, or the artist, the point can be recast as the question of the artist and her degree of density or presence in the work. One of the more consolidated ideas underpinning the production of Western art is that

36 On the semantic distinction between post-avant-garde and neo-avant-garde see Foster (1994).

37 The issue of the cognitive possibilities connected to art is obviously quite broad and highly debated. For examples see Lamarque (2008) and Manuel Garcia Carpintero (2016).

there can be no artist without a work, from which it follows that the coming into being of a work, and in some cases its preservation, depends on the artist. The artist herself can be imagined in various ways—the romantic genius, the craftsman or smith, someone who works alone or supported by an entire factory. One of the more engaging questions in this regard, which falls within what I shall call the 'prejudice in favour of the artist', another concept so dear to Western art, is whether a work of art can exist without an artist. Let us look at an example.

The Homeric poems are universally believed to be part of the formative matter from which Western culture originated. Yet, it is now largely accepted that a form of conceptual parsimony lay behind the attribution of the works to a single author, *Homer*. It is highly likely, in fact, that Homer never existed and that the Homeric poems were the expression of a sort collective creation, the perfect example of how a culture established itself by depositing its myths, learning, and knowledge in a series of stories that were only attributed to a single author, the poet-creator, *ex-post*. Hence, not only does it appear, in a sense, that we can have a work of art without an artist, but, more importantly perhaps, it appears that a narrative material that emerged without the explicit intentionality of an artist can become a work of art. The artist, in this case the poet, was perhaps necessary only to make the work emerge, to make the audience aware of it. Thus there exists a certain dependency of the work on the artist—the Homer or whoever in his stead grasped the foundational and mythical import of the stories and developed them—but it is, for all intents and purposes, a weak dependency. Homer, we said, may have never existed, or perhaps his role in the creation of the Homeric poems was much more marginal, or in any case different, than what his legacy suggests. Gianbattista Vico credits foundational poets such as Homer and Dante with the enormous merit of having given shape to the rather shapeless material produced by the peoples to which they belonged, which enabled those peoples to identify themselves with their language and their stories (Vico, Fisch, and Bergin 1948, Ch. XXV). The idea, therefore, that authorship is the outcome of shared or widespread practice, and that the author or artist gives shape to material that is sedimented in the collective memory of people, is, in a certain sense, of venerable age. That way of interpreting the work-artist relationship as a weak dependency greatly undermines the prejudice in favour of the artist, and instead promotes a distributed and shared concept of authorship and the notion of 'collective author', which in the history of art has remained somewhat implicit.

On the other hand, we have the notion of the artist as conceived by Romanticism, which did much to reinforce the prejudice in favour of the artist. The Romantic artist expresses the very essence of individuality as creative genius. Romanticism, therefore, shifted the theoretical framework for understanding the question of authorship, binding it to the idea of genius, absolute creativity, and uniqueness. Those properties, which identify the maker-creator, were then transposed on the work, which in turn became a unique object, an irreproducible one of a kind—an object bearing the aura theorized by Walter Benjamin. In the Romantic understanding of the subject, an art work has a strong dependence on its maker.

Contemporary art, in its various expressions, extensively explores the idea of authorship and the kind of dependency linking the artist to the art work. In participatory art performances, for instance, the artist is reminiscent in a certain sense of the Homeric poet, given that the work emerges from the collaboration of all the people involved in the performative work, who are not necessarily artists in the traditional sense of the term, namely, the sense expressed by the prejudice. It is the paradigm of the artist and his workshop that is transformed. Or, as with collective works, the idea of the artist, understood as a single creator, is deconstructed and replaced with a very different idea of subject. Oda Projesi[38] is an art collective of three Turkish artists, who began working together in 1997 from a three-room apartment in Istanbul. The collective's idea was to organize activities involving people from the neighbourhood, creating a space for engagement and dialogue, motivated by the need for integration. Practices of such a kind clearly show an attempt to minimize authorship and the aura surrounding the Romantic idea of authorship. In contrast with the Homeric poems, in the case of collectives such as Oda Projesi, the hand of the artists, in the sense of the artistic intentionality aimed at creating a work of art, is seen at the origin of the process, rather than at the end. Creation is effectively participatory, in the sense that people external to the collective contribute in a major way to making the work, in ways that cannot be reduced merely to production or material execution. Thus we have a decentralized idea of authorship which is especially marked, given that, more than with other art collectives, in the case of the three Turkish artists the work is the outcome of horizontal participation.

At the other end of the continuum constituting the concept of artist we have artists such as Andy Warhol, Joseph Beuys, and Marina Abramović, who stress how their works are dependent on their personality. In that regard, Warhol's use of a piece of packaging designed by James Harvey and presented, without any major changes, to the world of art as *Brillo Box*, declaring it his own work of art, is exemplary. The same can be said of Duchamp's ready-mades.

38 For more information on the collective's activities see http://odaprojesi.blogspot.it (last access: 10.06.2017).

Authorship, therefore, is a concept that has known many variations. It can be more or less dense, just as the dependency of works on their makers can be more or less rigid, but it does not appear possible to have a work without a maker, in the sense that the maker, whether a person or a collective, is always present at the start or the end of the creative process.

Similarly, however, it does not seem to make much sense for a work to be without an audience—the second meaning of 'subject' that we identified for our discussion. Even the audience, a sort of collective subject, has been interpreted and understood in various different ways by artists. Learned, distracted, generalist, specialist, educated or to be educated, enthusiastic or to be enthused, purified, or moved emotionally—whatever the collective subject for whom the musician composes, the artist paints, the writer writes, or the collective performs, the audience has to be there because it is to the audience that artistic communication is directed. The concept of audience underlying a certain artistic production has deeply influenced the kind of function and purpose associated with the arts over the centuries. Ultimately, what you do with art depends very much on the audience destined to receive a particular form of art.[39] The contemporary artworld finds itself dealing with a mass audience, in the sense that the power of the media through which the arts are distributed, or archived in some form—think of the widespread reach of the Web and applications such as iTunes, YouTube, or Art Stor—has rendered the traditional concept of audience as a circumscribed and determinate community way too restrictive. Millions of people with access to technologies that are now widespread can watch any movie they like, listen to any music track they like, peruse extraordinarily rich archives, and view from the comfort of an armchair countless pictures of such high definition that the virtual viewing experience of the *Mona Lisa*, say, or Botticelli's *Primavera* is arguably much better than at the Louvre or the Uffizi Gallery. It is patently obvious that listening to a Chopin Variation from a mobile device in our pocket, perhaps while crossing the street on the corner of Broadway and 110th in Manhattan, is completely different to hearing the same piece in a concert hall. Out on the street, it will be a diversion from the background noise of New York traffic, while in the concert hall we generally will concentrate on the piece and focus, for instance, on its structure, on understanding its musical properties, or in general on all that falls within the artistic and aesthetic domain. Out on the street, the music serves as a distraction to keep us company, or to relax, while making our way through Manhattan. In the concert hall we consider it an object of

39 For an interesting analysis see "Contemporary Art and the Public" (1971).

significance that deserves special attention and which permits aesthetic and artistic experience.[40]

(3) *A space for possibility.* Works of art convey something in their own way. That is, in ways that depend directly on the medium, or the body of the work, which generally obliges a metaphorical structure to be privileged over other possible types of expression. Generally speaking, that means two things. First, that the space of signification of works is much broader, but at the same time less precise, than, for instance, philosophy or other disciplines that are chiefly based on argumentation. Such broadness implies a semantic vagueness which is intrinsic to the work, and it is what permits in practice broad room for interpretation.[41] That is why a work cannot be conceived without a body, because the body is the medium, or what conveys, by embodying the work, aboutness. In possessing aboutness, that peculiar characteristic of being about something, works of art also possess a semantic structure, which ultimately means they have a physical body that enables meaning to be conveyed. Thus we have two fundamental elements with regard to meaning: (a) the being of the work as being about something, which is what the work means; and (b) the manner, or the semantic structure, enabling it to signify what it signifies.

How a work of art signifies something is related to normativity, which is the set of usages, conventions, rules, and technical means that make expression possible. Normativity is a necessary condition for art, even in the mechanisms and forms of deconstruction so dear to the historic avant-gardes, because all that needs or urges to be expressed requires the identification of a form and languages that enable signification. Even the most cryptic and enigmatic of expressions are constructed by means of a code that can be deciphered, in order for it to be possible to understand their meaning. But while means of signification concern normativity, meaning per se concerns two spheres, the sphere of sense and the sphere of emotions, which, according to some theories (Nussbaum 2001), and in the intuition of the writer, may very well overlap much more than common sense would normally suggest.

A comparative analysis can help clarify the idea. For the sciences, for example, meaning is what is acquired through method. Method implies the possibility of falsifying the meaning postulated in the experimental hypothesis. That typically does not happen in art, however, as since the work conveys aboutness, nobody would ever bother to produce a falsification. The artist can always make a work be about whatever he chooses it to be about, and no critical apparatus can insist on the illegitimacy of that act. Even where the aboutness

40 See, for example, Dewey (1954).

41 On this point see Eco (1989).

of a work is built on its close correlation with external reality (current affairs or history, for example) or with the internal reality of the artist (his unconscious, for instance), nobody can claim the legitimacy of a certain aboutness, as its aboutness is strictly dependent on its makers and on the fact it belongs to the fictional space of the work. Instead, art criticism generally focuses on the suitability or unsuitability of the medium, in the dual sense that it may not be suitable to express the meaning of the work (which may be the case for many various reasons), and hence it is not artistically appreciable, or it may not be of any particular significance from an aesthetic perspective. So while it is not within the rights of the artist to deprive a work of its artistic identity, or ultimately to restore the work to the sphere of non-being, the artist retains an absolute power over the domain of meanings he invests in a work, which are always true in an absolute sense. There are, however, two important exceptions to be made. The first is if internal consistency is lacking (an exception tied to the requirements of communication, for if internal consistency is lacking in a work, it cannot convey its meaning), while the second concerns the presence of inaccuracies in historic reconstructions, where such reconstructions are explicit and claimed to be such.

If, on the one hand, the structural form of meaning is fundamental for meaning to unfold, take shape, and be articulated, on the other it is also true that the arts—all of them—are not the same thing as philosophy. In other words, neither the form nor structure of its meanings coincide with the structure of logical thought expressed in the form of argument. We can assume, in fact, as various understandings of art do,[42] that artistic activity is a poietic activity, and hence preliminary to any activity that creates norms and values. Nevertheless, even from that point of view, the fact remains that art is interpreted as being a very different type of activity to all that which is constituted in logical thought. The question, therefore, is to identify the ways in which it is typified. I would like to suggest that those ways lie in the particular structure of what is generally classified as embodied meaning, or aboutness.

But first, I think it best to start with a preliminary consideration. Arguably, the term 'aboutness' is not perhaps the best description of the type of meaning we find embodied and displayed in art. Such a term, in fact, is limited in that, from a technical perspective, it only encompasses the semantic component of art, without sufficiently taking into consideration a question which I believe contemporary theories of art tend to neglect, namely, emotions. The semantic sphere is made up of two elements, meanings and emotions. It is significant how the first element, meaning, is given the connotation of moving

42 Vico (1948) significantly takes this approach.

predominantly in one direction, from the maker to the audience, while the second, emotions, is given the connotation of moving predominantly from the audience to the work. Then there is a fundamental distinction to be made, from an ontological perspective, concerning the question of time dependence. Meaning, in both its semantic and emotional components, is characterized differently depending on whether it is understood to unfold and be articulated and extended over time, or whether it is given in its entirety in a single temporal dimension. That is one of the differences that typically separate the visual arts from literature. A narrative that is given, so to speak, all at once in the circumscribed space of a canvas becomes time dependent only in the sense of the history of the interpretations and critical understandings of the work. It is only their stratification, therefore, that 'adds' something to the work over the course of time. Time is similarly a fundamental element when it comes to defining the nature of emotions which, in their more complex forms, need to be constructed and experienced through their unfolding over time. As such, let us imagine aligning emotions with the continuum that connects the arts. We see that the visual arts, as a whole, express a minimal emotional component, whereas literature, music, film, and the performing arts, in which extension in time is a constituent element of their identity, express time dependence in much more significant ways than the visual arts do.[43] If we accept that the semantic component of meaning cannot be disjoined from its emotional component, then it follows that each work will be the product of the unique balancing of these two elements and the ways in which the artist shapes them. Such a position lends itself particularly well to accounting for the tight compenetration that is found between meaning and emotion in literature.

A literary work embodies meanings of emotional connotation and it does so by recounting stories that, although narrated through the concrete portrayal of characters, aim in some way to exemplify universality. Such a strategy works particularly well in literature, where it is likely that compenetration is possible thanks to the extremely close link it has with the real world. In a certain sense, literature is also mimesis, although it is a mimesis that has nothing to do with being a pure mirror image. Literature does not duplicate the real world; if anything, it universalizes it and opens it to the dimension of the possible. But while the idea applies well to literature, it is objectively much more complicated to apply it other forms of art that show much looser ties to the real world. Here I refer chiefly to art forms that have a specifically weak tie to the real world, as in the case of abstract art (think of Pollock, for example) or conceptualism, or which appear to cut art off completely from the real world, as is

43 See on this Bell (1924) and Rosenberg (1983; 1964).

the case, for instance, in science fiction, both in literature and in film. Such art forms would appear to show how aboutness and emotions alone are not sufficient to explain how the arts manage to penetrate and give structure to the possible dimension, rendering it effectively accessible to us. If we accept that works of art possess aboutness (i.e., not just a meaning but, more specifically, a meaning structured in the form of aboutness), and that in certain types of art aboutness has an emotional connotation, or, vice versa, that the structure of a work is given by affectively-oriented thought, and hence by an aboutness which has an emotional connotation, then in many ways it is clear that the extension of aboutness over time is only made possible by the unfolding of a narrative structure.

From a structural perspective, emotions are kinds of relationships that motivate actions. Primary emotions (generally identified as anger, pleasure, pain, fear, and disgust) are elicited by various types of factors that are present, mostly, in the external world. Thus they are caused by the external world, which is true in the majority of cases, certainly in non-pathological cases. Nevertheless, it can happen that our innate disposition for empathy encourages us to participate in the emotional states experienced by others, by which we experience the emotions vicariously. To be empathically inclined towards somebody means being disposed to detecting a different emotional tone to our own in a certain moment and possibly sharing it, to the extent that it is caused by a person who is not us, but who occupies a place in our world. It also means being aware that at a certain time t, through an empathic relationship, we are experiencing an emotion or set of emotions vicariously.

It would be useful now, I believe, to distinguish the forms of art, and therefore the works of art, that possess an extension in time which enables them to construct and articulate a narrative structure that is accomplished with time and through time, and those which, on the contrary, possess an extension in time only because they perdure. Works that exist and perdure, whatever their ontology, have a structure that is compatible with time dependence. The hypothesis that I would like to introduce is that it is a time-dependent structure that depends on the structure of the work, but which in turn influences it in very clear ways. Thus I propose that time dependence in art can be understood in three different ways, specifically as structural time dependence, narrative time dependence, and, finally, interpretive time dependence. While structural time dependence is always present and is a necessary condition for the medium, whatever its ontology, to be given, narrative time dependence depends directly on the ontology of the work, in the sense that it is present and required by certain structures of work or certain types of works. In short, the *Divine Comedy* extends in time and that extension constitutes a part of the work itself, as it constitutes a necessary condition for the work to exist and for its narrative structure to unfold. Thus the *Divine Comedy*, like other, similar works, involves both a structural time dependence and a narrative time dependence. In contrast, *Guernica* possesses a semantic structure that involves time dependence, but only structural time dependence, which enables the work to perdure in time without involving or requiring a narrative time dependence. Finally, there is the third conception of time dependence, a time dependence that is external to the work and which involves and enables the archaeological stratification of interpretations to be formed. Both the *Divine Comedy* and *Guernica* give rise to a temporal dimension connected with how the work is received, enabling understandings and interpretations to condense around the work, which enrich the range of interpretations that the work can be given.

Let us recapitulate. The underlying idea is that both the *Divine Comedy* and *Guernica* possess aboutness, as both are undeniably about something. The *Divine Comedy* is about what we call life, its values, its possibilities, the ways in which we judge life, and the ways in which we live life, its passions, and its temptations. *Guernica*, on the other hand, is about war, human aggressiveness, and the ways in which we sometimes, and quite dramatically, are overcome by it. However, the way their meanings are conveyed to the audience, in each of the two cases, is typically different. Dante leads us, quite literally, on a journey that is substantiated and represented through the use of stories and characters that embody, in their eternal punishments, the very sense of their lives. Guilt sums up and hypostasizes the meaning of life, and exemplifies it through an interpretive act, Dante's, which in its own way is quite violent. For that guilt to be told, faults are given a specific emotional tone and are related to the audience through the sins they represent and through the emotional tones characterising each fault. Those faults, therefore, simplify and eternalize an existence, confining it to a single interpretation, Dante's, whose act of narration is also one of judgement—as though he had the knowledge of the Omniscient Narrator of Dantean memory.[44] Thus there is an emotional tone that identifies the author, who is also the narrating character, each character, each of the characters who interact with Dante, and, finally, the *Divine Comedy* as a whole. Two forms of time dependence are shown, a structural time dependence and a narrative time dependence, which enable the work to unfold and have the aboutness it has. As happens in empathic relationships, when we read the *Divine Comedy* or observe *Guernica*, we are aware of the emotional tone that attaches to our experience of the works, and we are aware, above all, that those emotions, complex and various as they are with the *Divine Comedy*,

44 See Danto (1968a).

simpler, and more linear and essential with *Guernica*, are guided by the wishes of the artist, and hence they are, in a sense, vicarious. The artist guides us in feeling them in the way he wants us to feel them. They belong to the artist or, rather, to the characters, and not to us, because they are emotions we feel vicariously. What is asked of us, as readers, observers, or users, is to be open to receiving them, to experiencing the emotions that Dante and Picasso relate, to be willing to make them ours and take them as our guide, and ultimately be moved to act by them.

We saw that to feel empathy means to feel, vicariously, the same or a similar emotion experienced by another person. That is true in ordinary life. In literature, the relationship between the author and the audience is conveyed essentially by two elements: *the fictional characters*, which are constructed by the author, but which in a certain sense elude the author in part as they open up a horizon of possibilities connected with the space for interpretation and emotive response of the reader, which goes beyond the total control of the author; and *the fictional marker*, which ties the work to the appropriated normative dimension, as the space of the work is a fictional space, carved out from the wider space of reality. That, or rather, the fact that the reader is able to grasp that in a simple and linear way, is what makes the reader's response to the vicarious emotions of the work different to the response that would be forthcoming if those same emotions were elicited within a non-fictional situation. Now, it is rather evident that the *Divine Comedy*'s unfolding over time permits Dante to explore a whole range of plot devices, details, and analyses that simply are not available to Picasso, who instead builds extensively on the imagination of his audience to elicit vicarious emotions in them. Those emotions, however, are necessarily less complex, as the narrative space of his figurative discourse offers fewer possibilities for articulation than literature, or even music, does. The unfolding of a work in time gives emotions the chance to assume a more multi-dimensional[45] and complex structure. Let us take empathy, for example. That empathy is interpreted, on the whole, as being a multi-dimensional disposition means, generally speaking, that various stimuli can elicit an empathic reaction. A reaction can be caused, for instance, by a certain situation, by a symbolic universe, or by the facial expression of the person we interact with. Moreover, cognitive processes, in this context, play a key role, as do references to past experience. In the case of art, vicarious emotions are elicited not by a person in flesh and blood but by "things that pretend to be people" (Ferraris 2012), that is, works. Outside of metaphor, that means that works of art are things that are able, by their very ontological structure, to elicit an emotional

45 For more insight on this see the theory developed by Hoffman (2001).

response in us. And they do so, in general, not simply by eliciting primary emotions—pain, pleasure, disgust, fear, and anger—but by making it possible for variously complex emotional states to be created, which require sophisticated cognitive ability and development to be both felt and understood.

Let us return to the *Divine Comedy* for a moment. We said how the work opens up a fictional space in which readers are exposed to feeling a series of vicarious emotions. In other words, they are true emotions elicited by the work and constructed, in the way they are constructed, by the author. The *Divine Comedy* is truly illustrative in this sense. Consider the eighth canto of the *Inferno*. Dante, led by the ever-vigilant and wise Virgil, is about to enter the City of Dis, which lies at the lower part of hell. Dis is described as a walled city of ferrous appearance, surrounded by the Styx, a slimy river in which certain lost souls, the wrathful, are immersed to atone for their sin. To reach Dis, Dante and Virgil need to cross the Styx, ferried by the boatman Phlegyas, a mythological character whom Dante transforms into a demon. The episode is skilfully constructed, with an emotional tenor that verges on tension, something that is felt from the very start of the canto when Dante and Virgil eye two flames of light in the distance, which are used to signal their arrival. The atmosphere is one of wait, the same that hovers over an army encampment and which marks the vigilant nights of the soldiers. The suspense that Dante creates at the start of the canto is broken by the arrival of Phlegyas, the wrathful demon tasked with ferrying the two poets across the river and who demands Dante's soul. Virgil is firm in his opposition, however, implying to him that Dante will not remain in that place. At that point, Dante describes a sudden change of scene. All of a sudden a soul emerges from the Styx, covered in slime and unrecognizable. It is one of the damned, who in his impertinence and arrogance demands to know who Dante is. The poet recognizes him immediately, despite his seriously compromised appearance, and specifically avoids revealing his name.

> "Who are you?" / cried a muddy shape that lifted up its head, / "who come down here before your time is due?" / "If I come, it is not to stay here with the dead. / But who are you, so covered with this mess?" / "You see that I am one who weeps," he said. / And I: "In weeping and in wretchedness / may you remain, damned soul, for even when / you are bathed in filth, I know you nonetheless.[46]

46 All quotes from the edition, Alighieri, Dante. 2003. *Inferno: A New Verse Translation by Michael Palma*, trans. M. Palma, New York: Norton (pp. 83–84).

The dialogue is a pressing crescendo. Filippo Argenti approaches Dante showing an arrogance that represents the justification for his punishment. A fearful Dante recognizes the damned soul and reiterates his judgement of him by hailing the justness of the punishment inflicted on him. The significance of his having recognized him, despite his murky aspect, can only aggravate that punishment, and, indeed, his recognition of him provokes the wrath of Argenti, who attempts to grab hold of the boat carrying the two poets.

> He stretched his two hands toward the boat just then, / but my wary master gave him a sharp thrust, / saying: "Back down with the other dogs again!" / Then he put his arms around my neck and kissed / my face. "Indignant soul," he said to me, / "the mother who carried you is truly blest! / In the world he was so arrogant. To his memory / not a scrap of goodness clings, so his spirit stays / down in the mire seething furiously. / How many who think themselves great kings these days / will lie like pigs in the muck here, and they will / leave behind names of horrible dispraise."

The changes in tone, from an emotional perspective, are clear to see. Filippo Argenti is enraged by Dante's reaction and tries to grab hold of the boat in a likely effort to make the two poets suffer his same fate. In doing so, he demonstrates once again in those circumstances the dominant trait of his character, a trait that has destined him for eternity to his punishment. Virgil responds to Argenti's ire with equal, if not perhaps a more violent wrath—not only does he push him away, but he apostrophizes him, calling him a dog. Another change of scene and we find Virgil addressing Dante with great tenderness, as he explains to him how Argenti's pride has proved so self-defeating. The souls on earth who are glorified for futile reasons are destined to suffer for eternity like "pigs in the muck". Dante's response comes with yet another change of tone and is surprising in some ways. Dante shows no sign of pity or indulgence towards Argenti, as though to signify that no indulgence is possible or due for such a sin—on the contrary, Dante rubs in the point by requesting that his desire for revenge find satisfaction.

> "Master," I said to him, "while we are still / on the lake, it would please me greatly if I might / see him dipped once more into the swill." / And he: "Before the shore has come in sight, / you will have satisfaction straightaway. / To grant a wish like that is only right."

While Argenti's wrath, combined with his pride, is deserving of eternal punishment, Dante is clearly of a different view with regard to his own desire for revenge, which (as the narrator) he completely indulges and satisfies.

> And soon the muddy mob began to flay / the shade so wildly that for what I saw / I still give thanks to God to this day. / "Let's get Filippo Argenti!" came the raw / cry of the crowd, and the raging Florentine / turned his teeth upon himself and began to gnaw.

Wrath, often paired with pride, is a cardinal sin. And wrath can only be met with wrath, as Virgil shows, presumably on the rationale that such a sentiment needs to be struck down with equally decisive and contrary force. The desire for revenge, on the other hand, which is what prompts Dante in wishing to see his enemy humiliated, instead deserves to be satisfied and fulfilled, in what seemingly appears to be the only direct amends that Argenti can offer the poet. Dante truly is not only *autor*, but also *auctoritas*, and his judgement condemns Argenti to eternal punishment, while he absolves himself by declaring his thirst for revenge to be perfectly legitimate. The canto ends with yet another change of emotional tone, as we are described a fearful Dante, distressed at the prospect of being abandoned by Virgil at the gates of Dis.

Dante constructs a world populated with historical figures from the living memory of his contemporary readers, and with the stroke of his pen he binds them to the sin that alone determines the meaning of their entire lives. And then, to add bite to his judgement and more effectively move our souls to action, he tells us not only what to think, but even how and what to feel in the face of those sins and judgements. As absolute judge, the poet dictates our own judgements and substantiates those judgements by steering us to feel appropriately. The *Divine Comedy* reflects the tragedy of the human condition, our weaknesses, vices, and failures, so in a way it is certainly true that it is mimetic in imitating life. Yet it is also true that the story, in contrast with the reality of daily life, is written by a single hand, which substantiates not only the author's own vision of the world, but also his judgement of it. Our response to the tales of the *Divine Comedy*, in relation to the judgements given but also the meanings and emotions conveyed, is a response to Dante and his world, which for us is made up of thoughts, judgements, and vicarious emotions. We know that in a certain way it all belongs to Dante, to his relationship with writing and with the real, yet at the same time fictitious characters, and to his desire to build an exemplary vision of the world. Yet, we generally respond to the work as though we were responding to a new world into which we step, by the kind concession of the author, and which becomes a sort of surrogate for the ordinary world. Typically, that is how literature affects us. The fictional marker is clear—we know it is all make-believe and that Dante is its absolute creator—yet the narrative, as it unfolds over time, weaving motives and judgements around the lives, both imaginary and plausibly true, of the characters, moves us to judgement, to indignation over injustices, to pity, and at times even induces us to stand apart emotively from the sentiments that Dante invites us to feel. It moves us emotively to respond to a fictional world and to compare that fictional world to the real world, and it is on that level that the shift occurs from the sphere of judgement, with its emotional connotations, as Nussbaum suggests, to the sphere of action proper.

By the end of the story, we have travelled across a possible world, playing by the rules that Dante sets us, or simply suggests; we have learnt to judge the way he judged and to contest in some cases his judgements; and finally we have aligned his world against our own, his idea of humanity against our own, and we have reformulated our idea of humanity in the light of his values, measuring them against ours. For all that to be possible, time was needed for the story to unfold and develop its wealth of details and properties, and the abundance of description and emotions which Dante describes and ascribes to his characters. The world of literature is a domain which extends in time and is constructed step by step, which expands progressively to occupy the space of the possible, and which grants no small room for the imagination. All of which implies a huge difference compared, for instance, to the domain of the visual arts.

(4) *The fictional marker and potential space.* That works of art are generally distinguished by a fictional marker, implying the need to differentiate them, from a cognitive and emotional perspective, from the real world in general, is clear and in a certain sense a truism, especially with the more traditional arts. The fictional marker can be either internal or external to the work. What matters is not so much where the artist places it, but whether she chooses to make it clearly perceptible and recognisable or not. The fictional marker generally has a standard structure in the various arts, but the structure is sufficiently flexible to allow for a great number of interesting variations.

Among the more theoretically compelling discussions that have emerged regarding the fictional marker, of particular interest is the observation of the function and structure of the chorus in classical theatre. The chorus has captured the attention of many thinkers for the enigma that surrounds its function, as it is not immediately clear what the purpose was that it served. The insights of that debate were notoriously gathered and discussed by Friedrich Nietzsche in *The Birth of Tragedy*. Before being considered a fictional marker, the chorus was seen to be the origin of tragedy itself, in the sense that originally, tragedy coincided with the chorus. The theories that followed then interpreted the chorus in essentially two different ways: as either the ideal spectator of the tragedy, or as the representative of the people before the king. The idea that the chorus served the function of ideal spectator was put forth by Schlegel. The second idea instead provides an interpretation of a political nature, which was discussed by Aristotle. Nietzsche completely rejected both interpretations on the grounds that they were unfounded. Schlegel's theory leads us to absolutize the audience, implying the paradox of an audience without a work of art as a consequence. On the other hand, the idea of assigning the chorus a political function, or the function of political representation, appeared quite simply implausible to Nietzsche on historical grounds, or rather, on the grounds of contemporary historical knowledge of the classical world and its culture. Nietzsche, however, found Schiller's theory interesting, which considers the chorus to be like a living wall, a symbol which marked a clear separation:

> Schiller had already divulged an infinitely more valuable insight into the meaning of the chorus in the famous foreword to *The Bride of Messina*, where he viewed the chorus as a living wall which tragedy built around itself in order to shut out the real world and to protect its ideal ground and poetic freedom. [...] The introduction of the chorus is, for Schiller, the decisive step through which war with naturalism in art is openly and honestly declared.
>
> NIETZSCHE 2008, 44

Thus Schiller's idea, which Nietzsche substantially took up, was that the origin of tragedy is the chorus, or the dithyramb, and it is fair to believe that, by originating tragedy, the chorus delimited the space of meaning (and reality) separating tragedy from reality. In that sense, the chorus founds tragedy and makes it possible, and by doing so delimits the fictional space. The chorus delimits in the sense that it distinguishes what lies within and what lies without the fictional space. What is characteristic of what lies within is that it does not reflect reality, however much it may resemble it. The rules that apply within the fictional space are, therefore, not the same as those that apply outside that space. The task of the fictional marker—in this case, the chorus—is, therefore, to delimit and to signify. It delimits the space of the rules, and it signifies that those rules exist and that to understand the tragedy it is essential to understand the structure of its rules.

Unsurprisingly, therefore, Nietzsche concluded his inquiry into classical tragedy and its sudden end by attributing the blame for its disappearance to

Euripides. Euripides, he alleges, modified the rules, first and foremost by transforming the chorus, which led the fictional space to become a normative space at the same time, with the ultimate objective of structurally modifying tragedy. Euripides did three things to reduce the distinction between fiction and reality to a minimum (Nietzsche 2008, 63ff). First, he brought the performance of tragedy closer to descriptions of everyday life. Secondly, he instructed the audience on the tragedy, putting them in a position to understand its philosophy. And thirdly, he became a chorus leader, transforming the chorus into a tool of sorts for the development of the poet's argument. Before Euripides, the chorus essentially enabled the transfiguration of real space into functional space, which technically is what—as Danto effectively explains[47]—makes a work of art possible.

While classical tragedy, through the chorus, clearly highlighted both the meaning and the structure and function of the fictional marker, contemporary arts, on the other hand, have often worked on the fictional marker in an effort to reduce its perceptibility and obviousness to a bare minimum. A frame, a stage, the space delimited by a museum or a theatre, represent a distinct marker of separation, providing instructions to an audience that is suitably trained to grasp them. The same happens, paradoxically, in cases in which the fictional marker is dislocated, placed, as the case may be, in an eccentric space with respect to the work, or reduced to the point of being imperceptible, or restructured to the point of being unrecognizable. Such cases represent the more experimental work of the twentieth-century avant-gardes, which often sought to explore the limits separating reality from fiction. It is that limit that makes artistic transfiguration possible, while at the same time shaping its form and aspect. Where that limit is missing, or it cannot be grasped, art quite simply slides into reality, the transfiguration implodes, and the space of the possible goes back to being the space of reality. Where we are able to grasp the presence of the fictional marker, more or less two things happen. First of all, we get ready to activate precise cognitive skills. And secondly, we get ready to activate a certain emotional disposition. On the cognitive side, we prepare ourselves to relate to the meanings embodied in artistic media and to decipher the structure of the representation, as shaped within the specific medium. On the emotional side, we prepare ourselves to receive the vicarious emotions embodied and expressed by the works. In short, the fictional marker opens up an individual space, which is characterized by its own syntax, making a particular epistemology possible and, as Nussbaum points out (2001, 263ff.), encouraging

47 On this see Danto (1964; 1981).

a certain disposition towards the articulation of a possible dimension, which is how time dependence steps in and shapes the ontology of the works.

(5) *Normativity*. At first glance, the idea that normativity has anything to do with art, or with what we traditionally consider to be the outcome of a process of freedom and creation, may strike us as strange. In reality, the arts are essentially normative, in that they are intrinsically concerned with the question of the creation and application of norms, both as concerns the sphere of production and the sphere of the formulation of artistic judgement and critical judgement. The sphere of production is intrinsically tied to the ontology of the work, in such a way that variations in ontology will ultimately end up directly affecting the normativity that identifies a work. The sphere of the formulation of judgement is instead a different matter, requiring an inquiry into the relationships that exist between a work of art and aspects of the external world. Philosophy is very much a matter of judgement. Aesthetics and philosophy of art deal, among their various matters, with the judgement of taste, that is, how beauty is distinguished from ugliness based on a definition of beauty. That is the case, at least, when philosophers work on definitions. If, instead, as sometimes happens, they choose to work outside of definitional issues, judgement is essentially a way of identifying analogies between, say, two similar objects. In that case, judgement is the identification of certain properties—such as those that distinguish works of art—and the verification of whether something does indeed have such properties. Framed that way, the issue seems rather simple. In fact, on the methodological level, the point would be to trace a particular case back to a general one; to identify the shared properties of two similar objects; or to identify the properties of a class of objects, art works, say, to decide what belongs to that class and what does not.

Traditionally, when an artist paints a picture, she expects it to be judged beautiful. At a historical time like our own, where beauty in art is not considered necessary, she might expect it to be considered a work of art despite its lack of beauty. What does that mean? As a first consideration, it could be argued that the artist expects agents of the art world, that is, those with an institutional mandate to act within it, to judge her work as legitimately belonging to the artworld. To do so it is not necessary for them to commit to the existence of a universal such as 'work of art', but it is necessary to believe that a certain classification grasps some characteristics that an object must have to be judged a work of art. In that sense, for example, it was long believed that works of art, to be such, had to exhibit characteristics such as the imitation of reality and beauty. That meant that objects created with explicit imitative aims and which were well made, with nicely matching colours, proportionate shapes, or given stylistic characteristics, were judged to belong to the domain of artistic production. Such an assumption implies the application of a normativity aimed at the formulation of judgement. So that the judgement is not continuously revised, it is necessary, where possible, that the framework is clear, that the definition is shared, and that normativity—the set of boundaries regulating the formation of judgement—is agreed upon. In this framework, what is interesting from a philosophical point of view is when for some reason the process breaks down, that is, it entails problems or even appears impossible. That is indeed the case with contemporary art as, for almost a century now, it has been revising its identity and therefore the artistic judgements made of its works.

Art is known to have a very long tradition. Arguably its best known narrative tends to trace that tradition back to a single process, which consists, roughly speaking, of changes mainly in technique and style. When we speak of art history, we refer to a process of change, not necessarily in terms of progress, that has affected the techniques and practices we attribute to art. The first and perhaps most important theoretical narration of art is that offered by Giorgio Vasari in his *Lives Of The Most Eminent Painters Sculptors And Architects* (Vasari 1979). Vasari thought that art progressed in terms of technical improvement and that the goal of art was essentially to resemble reality as closely as possible, improving its mimetic ability. The more an artist could imitate the external world in a realistic and precise manner, the more skilled he was considered to be and the more his works were considered canonical, that is, endowed with the paradigmatic function of *exempla*. The idea that the main goal of art was to imitate reality thus functioned as a norm for judgement, and that norm, despite the many changes that took place in the artistic canon, was long the criterion for critical judgement. Vasari's artistic ideal was that of the imitation of nature, as emerges from his description of Leonardo da Vinci's works, in which he notes, among other things, how they improved on the traditionally flat representation of figures:

> Leonardo then made a picture of Our Lady, a most excellent work, which was in the possession of Pope Clement VII; and, among other things painted therein, he counterfeited a glass vase full of water, containing some flowers, in which, besides its marvellous naturalness, he had imitated the dew-drops on the flowers, so that it seemed more real than the reality.
>
> VASARI 1979, 59

After Leonardo, or rather after Leonardo introduced very significant technical innovations, painting meant painting his way, reaching his technical ability in the imitation of nature and, at the same time, the ability to render that process in personal ways. Vasari thus constructed a rather organic narrative in which concepts such as 'work of art', 'beauty', 'imitation', 'portrait', and 'likeness' were enriched and complicated due to the characteristics and specificities of Leonardo's work. All that helped give aesthetic judgement a further dimension, implying, as an indirect consequence, more and better defined characteristics for aesthetic normativity. And it was thanks to the continuing expansion of artistic production that Vasari's narrative, which over time became the narrative and the normative canon of reference for the artworld, survived over the centuries, up to the threshold of the twentieth century. By providing the conceptual tools and theoretical basis for people in the artworld to formulate both expert and amateur judgements on how we understand, interpret and evaluate a given artwork, Vasari's canon, along with the normativity it produced and reinforced, worked rather well for a long period of time. The canon, therefore, made it possible to formulate a judgement in a simple and almost automatic way, based on the conviction that once the concept of reference is defined, it is possible to include in the canon all the works that can be retraced to the canon itself. The more precisely the canon is defined, the more it can facilitate the formulation of judgements. Now, it is surely interesting to understand the structure and functioning of judgement, but it is even more interesting to see what happens when those mechanisms do not work, that is, when the canon does not enable the formulation of an ordinary judgement, either because it is too broad or because it is challenged by something radically new.

That is what happened in the second half of the twentieth century, when Western artists began producing works that hardly fit the established canon. Abstract art had already put Vasari's canon—the idea that art has a mainly mimetic purpose—to the test, but it was the introduction of ready-mades, that is, ordinary objects, into the world of art that marked the definitive and complete breakdown of the traditional idea of art. Seeing as such objects required no artistic technique or practice, the canon clearly could not explain their production. Vasari's canon had withstood a number of variations, maintaining its effectiveness, but now it proved insufficient to formulate aesthetic-artistic judgements. The production of ready-mades demanded a radical revision of artistic judgement, both by experts and by ordinary folks. The impossibility of using the traditional canon to formulate the judgements required by the artworld led to the practical need to reconsider the canon itself in full. As the philosophy of art of the late twentieth century shows, the point was no longer simply to adjust Vasari's canon to justify the inclusion of some specific works, but rather to reformulate the canon completely. What was needed was a theoretical analysis based on the ontology of art that would give a new answer to the question, 'What is art?' Cases had arisen that had created a clean break with the canon, such that the conditions allowing for the formulation of judgement were no longer valid after them. *Bird in space* was one such case, a sculpture devoid of any mimetic character—at most it captures some properties that are typical, but secondary, of the represented object. In other words, *Bird in Space* formally and visually renders some traits, which are not immediately obvious at a perceptive level, of the idea of a bird flying through space—a lightness recalling weightlessness, and a tapered shape that can cleave the air. That set of formal and ideal, rather than aesthetic, properties comes into play in the formulation of a judgement that has to be ontological-artistic first (that is, it has to formulate arguments based on which the object can be recognized as a work of art, thereby inserting it in the same class as Donatello's *David*) in order to allow for aesthetic judgement (through which the quality of the work is judged). Hence the obvious impossibility of formulating, in the case of *Bird in Space*, an ontological-artistic judgement, which resulted in the impossibility of classifying the object as belonging to the sphere to which its maker assigned it. The outcome was a short circuit of such magnitude as to involve a fundamental rethinking of judgement applied to the sphere of art.

The visual arts of the twentieth century raised a number of issues concerning the formulation of judgements. Those issues included: (1) the fact that elements influencing judgement have their own specific weight, with some being more important than others; (2) the fact that those elements are identified, selected, and ordered by people who have the authority to do so (the agents of the art world, for example, who, in various ways, deal with different aspects of that world); and finally, (3) the fact that each domain enables a hierarchy in the formulation of judgements. For contemporary art, the formulation of an ontological-artistic judgement comes before the formulation of aesthetic judgement, which is entirely different from what occurred in the context of Vasari's tradition. Let us look at these points in more detail, working backwards from (3), that is, from the hierarchization of judgements. With traditional art, identifying a work of art is hardly a matter of discussion—the basic structural characteristics of a painting or a sculpture are not hard to identify. At most, debates have centred on forms of expression considered 'borderline', such as rock paintings or Russian icons, the former being perhaps devoid of artistic intentionality, the latter having been conceived originally as sacred objects. With contemporary visual arts, the issue is much more complicated, as their fictional markers—the things marking the space in which the work exists—are often placed in the background or made almost imperceptible.

That has allowed artists to play on the weakening of the presence, first at the perceptual level and then at the cognitive level, of the fictional spaces that identify works of art. In such cases, the ontological-artistic judgement can obviously only precede the aesthetic judgement. The point is that a work of art must first be recognized as such, by differentiating it from its non-artistic counterparts.

What I have just described is a hierarchical organization of judgements related to the domain of art that allows for the existence of the domain itself. Once again, it is interesting to look at those cases where artists have complicated the hierarchy of fundamental judgements in the domain of art. Consider performances that seek to confuse ordinary action and artistic action. The aim is precisely to make us reflect on the domain of action, compelling us to a twofold task: first, to think about the specific characteristics of artistic action; second, to examine the genuine content of the action that we are observing and that we are called to classify as artistic action. The most obvious consequence of such practices is that most of the time the formulation of artistic judgement is made impossible or very difficult, especially without a visible fictional marker. Given that the fictional marker is placed in the background and made imperceptible,[48] the performer works on the reaction of the audience, which varies also depending on whether the spectator can distinguish the artistic action from an ordinary one. Being on all fours to clean a church hall may be a routine action for a cleaner, but when that action is performed by a performer, without any fictional marker being used explicitly to distinguish the artistic action—i.e., an action with a different meaning despite fully taking on the structure of an ordinary action—from ordinary action, we can be certain that the audience will find it greatly difficult to classify the action in question correctly. In such situations, the audience's judgement is structured in the same way as it would be for everyday actions unrelated to art. An action, or a series of actions, can usually be judged in an ethical, moral, or practical sense—it is relatively rare that our judgements of actions involve aesthetics. Hence, with artistic performances, the absence of a fictional marker—be it a museum, a theatre, or something hinting at the presence of an art work—deters the audience from looking for the properties they would usually attribute to works of art. Since the performance consists of the representation of a certain action through the properties that identify the action as ordinary, while at the same time lacking any marker that would enable the audience to grasp the identifying properties of the artistic object, the audience may fail

48 For a more in-depth analysis of the role of fictional markers see Andina (2013).

to make the ontological judgement and be unable to identify the work appropriately, or may suspend judgement for a time. If it is radically impossible to formulate an ontological-artistic judgement, the artist will have somehow failed, as no one else will recognize the work as art. It is therefore evident that, to avoid such a situation, contextual properties are needed in addition to aesthetic ones.

The second point (2) in our list of issues raised by contemporary visual arts focuses on the issue of who may choose the elements (properties, characteristics, qualities, and so on) which underpin the normativity of judgements in the domain of art. The question is clearly a delicate one, which often depends on the specific context of art. The fundamental point is that such judgements are legitimately formulated not only by experts or people fully informed on the matter in question, but also by non-experts—and their opinions often differ significantly. Therefore, there are two issues to be addressed. The first relates to the legitimacy of the judgement of non-experts, which, in some contexts, can play a very significant role, sometimes showing a close dependence on the market. Think of how often we read about a work being perfectly snubbed by the critics, but received with great acclaim by the general public, that is, by people who are not trained to be competent professionally in relation to the domain of art. In reality, the judgement of non-experts in the domain of art has always contributed significantly to shaping expert opinion, so that the sphere of art is very receptive and open to novelty. Various art movements—think of Pop Art, for instance—specifically questioned the distinction between high art and low art, which for a long time underpinned a good part of art theory, and sought to spread the arts as much as possible by producing art works able to please less sophisticated tastes.

Significantly, the origin of the term 'Impressionism' goes back to Louis Leroy's critical review of Claude Monet's *Impression, Soleil Levant* (1872) for the newspaper *Le Charivari*. It was in defiance of the dismissive use of the term by the critic—an expert agent of the artworld—that the group of artists chose to defines themselves as 'Impressionists', co-opting his critique as the best description of their poetics and thereby decreeing a public and critical success that would secure the movement's place within the history of art. In the case of Impressionism, therefore, the judgement of the artists determined the prevailing attitude, reversing the judgement formulated by other agents of the art world. Yet that is not always the case—nor is it, ultimately, always a good thing. It is evident that in such a context, the question becomes who can formulate judgements and what are their basic normative structures. That is particularly clear in the *Brâncuși v. United States* case, where to clarify the issue of whether *Bird in Space* was or was not a work of art, various agents of the artworld were called to testify. In fields like the artworld, where the domain of reference is vague and rather unstructured, consensus and judgement appear to emerge according to dynamics that are not necessary or always foreseeable. Mostly, such dynamics are not driven by a single agent, or a single type of agent, nor by a single factor. It may be beauty that is privileged, or expressiveness, or, alternatively, the meaning of the work, but ultimately all those elements, understood and applied in different ways, can lead to radically different judgements.

It is therefore plausible to assume that most of the time aesthetic judgement is determined in a relatively accidental way, emerging rather randomly. Ontological-artistic judgement, conversely, seems to be more stable. Today, it is true, we are prepared to include chairs and urinals in a much broader class of works of art, one in which urinals exist *alongside* paintings, but that has only come after a complex re-determination of the ontology underlying artistic production. Such reconsiderations, however, demanded mainly by the artists themselves, can only happen rarely—otherwise the domain of art would risk disintegrating completely. As a first approximation, therefore, we can say that there are different sources of legitimacy for aesthetic judgement—experts, non-experts, more or less cultivated people, and so on, who, on the basis of largely indefinable variables, can play a potentially decisive role in market dynamics that often are influenced by economic factors. But when it comes to ontological-artistic judgement, it all depends on the artist. It was, after all, Duchamp—taking his ready-mades as our paradigmatic example—who decided that some properties (such as hand-made production, or aesthetic qualities) were less important than others (such as mass production) in determining the concept of the work of art. And it was by changing the balance of importance of those properties, by which they come to overshadow each other (beauty, for instance is certainly not the defining property of *Fountain* as an art work), that Duchamp contributed to creating a new, broader concept of art, one able to reveal a part of the domain of art that had yet to be explored.

Finally, let us turn to point one (1) of our list, which highlights how each of the elements that affect the formulation of judgement carry a specific weight. That means that not everything is equally important, and judgements can be formulated precisely because we are able to arrange the elements that make them up hierarchically. As I noted earlier, there are two kinds of judgement in the domain of art, ontological-artistic judgement and aesthetic judgement. As we have seen, the former makes the latter possible. With ontological-artistic judgement, which answers the question, 'What is art?', art in the twentieth century showed how it is affected varyingly by the physical properties of the object, its relational properties (the properties that depend on the relationship between work and artist, work and audience, and artist and audience), and its contextual properties (properties that depend on the historical and cultural context of the work).

As I have shown, artists can choose to expand that set of properties, to vary its relations, and to use them in very different ways. The fact that artistic production is in constant evolution, and therefore never completely standardized, means that the constant redetermination of which properties affect ontological-artistic judgement will persist as long as there is art. When variations are not extremely significant and concern marginal modifications within the established paradigm, the artist is not called to provide a theoretical justification for her choice; but when changes are substantial, a theoretical supplement is not only appropriate but often necessary. That theoretical basis then becomes the normative underpinning enabling the formulation of judgements in the ontological field.

Things are different when it comes to aesthetic judgement, (which concerns the aesthetic properties of art works). As suggested earlier, the audience, as well as art critics, art historians, gallery owners, and so forth, are probably those best entitled to judge the aesthetic quality of an art work. And they can do so on the basis of very different criteria, all of which are admitted, if not explicitly codified, by the artworld. In some cases what will prevail is refined and cultivated taste; in others it will be momentary fashion or reflect the needs of the market, or else show an interest in experimentation and aesthetic inquiry. The reasons why an audience determines the success of a given art work have changed significantly over time. In relatively recent times, technological progress and mass media have contributed profoundly to transforming the modes of production and experience of art. In such a context, it is quite evident that ontological-artistic judgements are generally better formulated and more normalized than aesthetic judgements, especially in periods when artistic production is relatively stable, or when artists do not introduce significant changes challenging the 'ontology of art'. Aesthetic judgements, conversely, depend primarily on how human perception is structured, and secondarily on how culture influences the enjoyment of art—to remain in relatively recent times, Impressionist art is exemplary in this sense. Finally, it depends on the dynamics of the market, which in some cases is able to bring a work of art to our collective attention and appreciation. In short, the formulation of aesthetic judgement is profoundly linked not only to our senses, but also to our value systems, both ethical and economic.

Bibliography

Abell, Catharine. 2012. "Art: What it Is and Why it Matters." *Philosophy and Phenomenological Research* 85 (3):671–691.

Abrams, M. H. 1953. *The Mirror and the Lamp: Romantic Theory and the Critical Tradition*. New York: Oxford University Press.

Alighieri, Dante, and Michael Palma. 2003. *Inferno: A New Verse Translation by Michael Palma*. New York: Norton.

Andina, Tiziana. 2011. *Arthur Danto: Philosopher of Pop*. Newcastle upon Tyne: Cambridge Scholars.

Andina, Tiziana. 2013. *The Philosophy of Art: The Question of Definition—From Hegel to Post-Dantian theories*. Translated by Natalia Iacobelli. Bloomsbury Studies in Philosophy. London: Bloomsbury.

Angelucci, Sergio. 1994. *Arte contemporanea, conservazione e restauro: contributi al "Colloquio sul restauro dell'arte moderna e contemporanea."* Fiesole (FI): Nardini.

Aristotle. 2007. *On Rhetoric: A Theory of Civic Discourse*. Translated by George A. Kennedy. 2nd ed. New York: Oxford University Press.

Austin, J. L. 1962. *How to Do Things with Words*. The William James Lectures. Oxford: Clarendon Press.

Auxier, Randall E., and Lewis Edwin Hahn. 2013. *The Philosophy of Arthur C. Danto*. The Library of Living Philosophers. Chicago: Open Court.

Batteux, Charles. 1746. *Les beaux arts reduits à un même principe*. Paris: Durand.

Baumgarten, Alexander Gottlieb. 1961. *Aesthetica*. Hildesheim: G. Olms.

Bell, Clive. 1924. *Art*. London: Chatto & Windus.

Belting, Hans, Andrea Buddensieg, and Peter Weibel. 2013. *The Global Contemporary and the Rise of New Art Worlds*. Karlsruhe, Germany, Cambridge, MA: ZKM/MIT Press.

Benjamin, Walter. 1963. *Das Kunstwerk im Zeitalter seiner technischen Reproduzierbarkeit; drei Studien zur Kunstsoziologie*. Frankfurt on Main: Suhrkamp Verlag.

Biro, Adam, ed. 2003. *Brancusi contre états-Unis. Un procès historique, 1928*. Paris: Adam Biro.

Bishop, Claire. 2005. "The Social Turn: Collaboration and its Discontents." *Artforum* 44 (6):178–183.

Bishop, Claire. 2012. *Artificial Hells: Participatory Art and the Politics of Spectatorship*. London: Verso Books.

Bourriaud, Nicolas. 2002. *Relational Aesthetics*. Dijon: Les Presses du réel.

Carrier, David, and Joachim Pissarro. 2013. *Wild Art*. London: Phaidon.

Carroll, Noèel. 2000. *Theories of Art Today*. Madison: University of Wisconsin Press.

Cohen, Ted. 1973. "The Possibility of Art: Remarks on a Proposal by Dickie." *The Philosophical Review* 82 (1):69–82. doi: 10.2307/2184239.

"Contemporary Art and the Public." 1971. *Leonardo* 4 (4):385–387. doi: 10.2307/1572518.

Crawford, Francine. 1975. "Pre-Constitutional Copyright Statutes." *Bullettin of the Copyright Society of the USA* 23.

Cross, Anthony. 2017. "Obligations to Artworks as Duties of Love." *Estetika: The Central European Journal of Aesthetics* LIV/2017:85–101.

Danto, Arthur. 1964. "The Artworld." *The Journal of Philosophy* 61 (19):571–584. doi: 10.2307/2022937.

Danto, Arthur. 1965. *Analytical Philosophy of History*. Cambridge: Cambridge University Press.

Danto, Arthur. 1968a. *Analytical Philosophy of History*. Cambridge: Cambridge University Press.

Danto, Arthur. 1968b. *Analytical Philosophy of Knowledge*.Cambridge: Cambridge University Press.

Danto, Arthur. 1973. *Analytical Philosophy of Action*. Cambridge: Cambridge University Press.

Danto, Arthur. 1981. *The Transfiguration of the Commonplace: A Philosophy of Art*. Cambridge, MA: Harvard University Press.

Danto, Arthur. 1986. *The Philosophical Disenfranchisement of Art*. New York: Columbia University Press.

Danto, Arthur. 1987. *The State of the Art*. New York: Prentice Hall Press.

Danto, Arthur. 1992. *Beyond the Brillo Box : The Visual Arts in Post-historical Perspective*. New York: Farrar Straus Giroux.

Danto, Arthur. 1997. *After the End of Art: Contemporary Art and the Pale of History*. The A W Mellon Lectures in the Fine Arts. Princeton, NJ: Princeton University Press.

Danto, Arthur. 2003. *The Abuse of Beauty: Aesthetics and the Concept of Art*. Paul Carus Lecture Series. Chicago: Open Court.

Danto, Arthur C., and ebrary Inc. 2009. "Andy Warhol." In *Icons of America*. New Haven: Yale University Press. http://www.columbia.edu/cgi-bin/cul/resolve?clio10590110.

Davies, Stephen. 2005. "Definitions of Art." In *Routledge Companion to Aesthetics*, edited by Berys Gaut and Dominic McIver Lopes, 227–39. London: Routledge.

Dewey, John. 1954. *Art and Education*, 3rd ed. Merion, PA: Barnes Foundation Press.

Dickie, George. 1969. "Defining Art." *American Philosophical Quarterly* 6 (3):253–256.

Dickie, George. 1974. *Art and the Aesthetic: An Institutional Analysis*. Ithaca, NY: Cornell University Press.

Dickie, George. 1984. *The Art Circle: A Theory of Art*. New York: Haven Publications.

Dickie, George, and Gerhard Charles Rump. 1978. "Art and the Aesthetic: An Institutional Analysis." *Leonardo* 11 (2):175–176. doi: 10.2307/1574067.

Dickie, George, and R.J. Sclafani. 1977. *Aesthetics: A Critical Anthology*. New York: St. Martin's Press.

Dimitrakaki, Angela, and Kirsten Lloyd. 2015. *Economy: Art, Production and the Subject in the Twenty-first Century* (*Value: Art: Politics*). Liverpool: Liverpool University Press.

Eco, Umberto. 1989. *The Open Work*. Translated by Anna Cancogni. Cambridge, MA: Harvard University Press.

Edelman, Bernard. 2011. *Tous artistes en droit : petite histoire de l'esthâetique á l'ére des droits de l'homme*. Paris: Hermann.

Ferraris, Maurizio. 2012. *La fidanzata automatica*. Milan: Bompiani.

Findlay, Michael. 2012. *The Value of Art: Money, Power, Beauty*. Munich: Prestel.

Foster, Hal. 1994. "What's Neo about the Neo-Avant-Garde?" *October* 70:5–32. doi: 10.2307/779051.

Freeland, Cynthia. 2001. *But Is It Art?* Oxford: Oxford University Press.

Gaut, Berys, and Dominic McIver Lopes. 2005. *The Routledge Companion to Aesthetics*. 2nd ed. London: Routledge.

Goehr, Lydia. 2007. *The Imaginary Museum of Musical Works: An Essay in the Philosophy of Music*, rev. ed. Oxford: Oxford University Press.

Goldsmith, Steven. 1983. "The Readymades of Marcel Duchamp: The Ambiguities of an Aesthetic Revolution." *The Journal of Aesthetics and Art Criticism* 42 (2):197–208. doi: 10.2307/430663.

Harries, Karsten. 2009. *Art Matters: A Critical Commentary on Heidegger's "Of The Work of Art"*. New York: Springer.

Hartshorne, Thomas L. 1986. "Modernism on Trial: C. Brancusi v. United States (1928)", *Journal of American Studies* 20, no. 1 (Apr. 1986):93–104

Heidegger, Martin. 1967. *Being and Time*. Translated by John Macquarrie and Edward Robinson. Oxford: Blackwell.

Heidegger, Martin. 2002. *Off the Beaten Track*. Edited and translated by Julian Young and Kenneth Haynes. Cambridge: Cambridge University Press. Originally published as *Holzwege*. Frankfurt on Main: V. Klostermann. 1950.

Heidegger, Martin. 2008. *Basic Concepts of Ancient Philosophy*. Translated by Richard Rojcewicz. Studies in Continental Thought. Bloomington: Indiana University Press.

Heidegger, Martin. 2012. *Contributions to Philosophy (Of the Event)*. Translated by Richard Rojcewicz and Daniels Vallega-Neu. Blooming: Indiana University Press.

Hobbes, Thomas. 1650. *De corpore politico. Or, The elements of the lavv, moral & politick. With discourses upon several heads; as of the law of nature. Oathes and covenants. Severall kind of government. With the changes and revolutions of them*. London: Printed for J. Martin, and J. Ridley.

Hobbes, Thomas. 2012. *Leviathan*. Edited by Noel Malcolm. 3 vols. The Clarendon Edition of the Works of Thomas Hobbes. Oxford: Clarendon Press.

Hoffman, Martin L. 2001. "Toward a Comprehensive Empathy-based Theory of Prosocial Moral Development." In *Constructive & Destructive Behavior: Implications for Family, School, & Society*, edited by A. C. Bohart and D. J. Stipek, 61–86. Washington, DC: American Psychological Association.

Irvin, Sherri. 2005. "The Artist's Sanction in Contemporary Art", *Journal of Aesthetics and Art Criticism* 63 (4):315–326.

Kant, Immanuel. 1995. "Sulla legittimità della riproduzione dei libri." In *Scritti di Storia, Politica, Diritto*, edited by Filippo Gonnella. Rome: Laterza.

Kant, Immanuel. 1996. "The Metaphysics of Morals (1797)." In *Practical Philosophy*, translated and edited by Mary J. McGregor, 353–604. Cambridge: Cambridge University Press.

Kennick, William E. 1958. "Does Traditional Aesthetics Rest on a Mistake?" *Mind* 67 (267):317–334.

Kester, Grant H. 2004. *Conversation Pieces: Community and Communication in Modern Art*. Berkeley: University of California Press.

Kieran, Matthew, and Dominic McIver Lopes, eds. 2007. *Knowing Art: Essays in Aesthetics and Epistemology*. Philosophical Studies Series 107. Dordrecht: Springer Netherlands.

Krauss, Rosalind E. 1999. "Reinventing the Medium." *Critical Inquiry* 25 (2):289–305.

Krauss, Rosalind E. 2000. *A Voyage on the North Sea: Art in the Age of the Post-Medium Condition*. London: Thames & Hudson.

Kristeller, Paul Oskar. 1951. "The Modern System of the Arts: A Study in the History of Aesthetics, Part I." *Journal of the History of Ideas* 12 (4):496–527. doi: 10.2307/2707484.

Lamarque, P. 2008. *The Philosophy of Literature*. Foundations of the Philosophy of the Arts. Chichester, UK: Wiley-Blackwell.

Lang, Berel, and Arthur C. Danto. 1984. *The Death of Art*. Art and Philosophy Vol. 2. New York: Haven.

Leonardo, Leon Battista Alberti, Raphael Trichet du Fresne, and Cosimo Bartoli. 1651. *Trattato della pittvra di Lionardo da Vinci, nouamente dato in luce*. Paris: Appresso Giacomo Langlois.

Levinson, Jerrold. 2015. *Musical Concerns: Essays in Philosophy of Music*. Oxford: Oxford University Press.

Levinson, Jerrold. 1979. "Defining Art Historically." *The British Journal of Aesthetics* 19 (3):232–250.

Levinson, Jerrold. 1989. "Refining Art Historically." *The Journal of Aesthetics and Art Criticism* 47 (1):21–33. doi: 10.2307/431990.

Levinson, Jerrold, ed. 2014. *Suffering Art Gladly. The Paradox of Negative Emotion in Art*. London: Palgrave Macmillan.

Lopes, Dominic McIver. 2007. "Art Without 'Art'." *British Journal of Aesthetics* 47 (1):1–15. doi: https://doi.org/10.1093/aesthj/ayl035.

Lopes, Dominic McIver. 2008. "Nobody Needs a Theory of Art." *The Journal of Philosophy* 105 (3):109–127.

Lopes, Dominic McIver. 2014. *Beyond Art*. Oxford: Oxford University Press.

Mandelbaum, Maurice. 1965. "Family Resemblances and Generalization concerning the Arts." *American Philosophical Quarterly* 2 (3):219–228.

Manuel Garcia Carpintero, ed. 2016. "Recent Debates on Learning from Fiction." *Teorema* 35 (3):5–20.

Monseré, Annelies. 2016. "Why We Need a Theory of Art." *Estetika: The Central European Journal of Aestetics* LIII/2:165–183.

Nanay, Bence. 2016. *Aesthetics as Philosophy of Perception*. Oxford: Oxford University Press.

Nietzsche, Friedrich Wilhelm. 2008. *The Birth of Tragedy*. Translated by Douglas Smith. Oxford World's Classics. Oxford: Oxford University Press.

Nietzsche, Friedrich Wilhelm. 1927. *Ecce Homo: and The Birth of Tragedy*. Translated by Clifton Fadiman. The Modern Library of the World's Best Books. New York: The Modern Library.

Nietzsche, Friedrich Wilhelm. 1997. *On the Genealogy of Morals. A Polemic, By way of clarification and supplement to my last book, Beyond Good and Evil*. Translated by Douglas Smith. Oxford World's Classics. New York: Oxford University Press.

Nussbaum, Martha Craven. 2001. *Upheavals of Thought: The Intelligence of Emotions*. Cambridge: Cambridge University Press.

Plato. 1993. *Republic*. Translated by Robin Waterfield. Oxford World's Classics. Oxford: Oxford University Press.

Pöggeler, O. 1987. *Martin Heidegger's Path of Thinking*. Translated by Daniel Margushak and Sigmund Barber. Leiden: Brill.

Poli, Francesco. 1975. *Produzione artistica e mercato*. Piccola biblioteca Einaudi 237. Turin: G. Einaudi.

Poli, Francesco. 2011. *Il sistema dell'arte contemporanea*. Rome: Laterza.

Ramljak, Suzanne, Michele Oka Doner, Morris Lapidus, and Arthur C. Danto. 2003. *Michele Oka Doner: Natural Seduction*. New York: Hudson Hills Press.

Rollins, Mark. 2012. *Danto and his Critics*, 2nd ed., Philosophers and their Critics. Chichester UK: Wiley-Blackwell.

Rosenberg, Harold. 1964. *The Anxious Object: Art Today and Its Audience*. New York: Horizon Press.

Rosenberg, Harold. 1983. *The De-definition of Art*. Chicago: University of Chicago Press.

Rowell, Margit, and Andrâe Paleologue. 1999. *Brancusi vs. United States, the Historic Trial, 1928*. Paris: Adam Biro.

Saw, Ruth. 1961. "What is a 'Work of Art'?" *Philosophy* 36 (136):18–29. doi: 10.1017/S0031819100057806.

Schapiro, Meyer. 1968. "The Still Life as a Personal Object—A Note on Heidegger and van Gogh." In *The Reach of Mind. Essays in Memory of Kurt Goldstein*, edited by Marianne L. Simmel, 203–209. New York: Springer.

Schopenhauer, Arthur. 2010. *The World as Will and Representation. Volume. 1*. Edited and translated by Judith Norman, Alistair Welchman, and Christopher Janaway. The Cambridge Edition of the Works of Schopenhauer. New York: Cambridge University Press.

Searle, John R. 1995. *The Construction of Social Reality*. New York: Free Press.

Shiner, L. E. 2001. *The Invention of Art: A Cultural History*. Chicago: University of Chicago Press.

Tatarkiewicz, Władysław. 1980. *A History of Six Ideas: An Essay in Aesthetics*, Melbourne International Philosophy Series. The Hague: Martinus Nijhoff.

Thomasson, Amie. 2005. "The Ontology of Art and Knowledge in Aesthetics." *Journal of Aesthetics and Art Criticism*, 63 (3):221–229.

Vasari, Giorgio. 1979. *Lives of the Most Eminent Painters, Sculptors, and Architects*. Translated by Gaston Du C. De Veres. 3 vols. New York: Abrams.

Vico, Giambattista. 1948. *The New Science of Giambattista Vico: Translated from the Third Edition (1744)*. Translated by Max Harold Fisch and Thomas Goddard Bergin. Ithaca, NY: Cornell University Press.

Weitz, Morris. 1956. "The Role of Theory in Aesthetics." *The Journal of Aesthetics and Art Criticism* 15 (1):27–35. doi: 10.2307/427491.

Wollheim, Richard. 1968. *Art and its Objects. An Introduction to Aesthetics*. New York: Harper & Row.

Young, James O. 2001. *Art and Knowledge*. London: Routledge.

Zarobell, John. 2017. *Art and the Global Economy*. Oakland, CA: University of California Press.

www.ingramcontent.com/pod-product-compliance
Lightning Source LLC
Chambersburg PA
CBHW031331230926
51848CB00001B/188
* 9 7 8 9 0 0 4 3 6 1 4 1 6 *